THE
SCIENCE
OF
CHECKERS AND DRAUGHTS

(BLACK)

(WHITE)

TERMS: White to play and win

One against many   **Courtesy** Norristown Times Herald

THE
SCIENCE
OF
CHECKERS
AND DRAUGHTS

Tom Wiswell

Free-Style World Champion

South Brunswick and New York: A. S. Barnes and Company

© 1973 by A. S. Barnes and Co., Inc.

B-2

A. S. Barnes and Co., Inc.
Cranbury, New Jersey 08512

Library of Congress Cataloging in Publication Data

Wiswell, Thomas.
    The science of checkers and draughts.

    1. Checkers. I. Title.
GV1463.W537   794.2   74-168372
ISBN 0-498-07932-5

Printed in the United States of America

Some of the Other Books by Tom Wiswell

Let's Play Checkers
Learn Checkers Fast
America's Best Checkers
World Championship Checkers
Checkers in Ten Lessons
Checker Magic
Challenge of Checkers & Chess
Checker Kings in Action
The Art of Checkers
International Draughts
Twentieth Century Checkers
Championship Checkers and Chess for All
The Complete Guide to Checkers
Chess (with Kenneth Grover)
Top Notch Checkers (Co-author)

The author gratefully dedicates this work to the following champions of checker science. Their star moves and sacrifices have made it a winner:

John Fursa	J. Robert Jackson
Parks Herzog	John Cary
J. Minshull	Emin Elam
J. Mitchell Ellis	Alan Millhone
Dr. Lewis F. Schreiber	W. B. Grandjean
Clayton Beebe	Howard Floyd
Robert Mesch	Earl Ingram
Dr. Julius Belinkoff	D. L. Costello
Anthony Petronella	Louis Burt
Bill Salot	Sam Frankel
Fred Kritzler	Walter Goldwalter
Joe Cinderella	Antonio F. Tammaro

Contents

Preface

My first book of end-games, *Checker Magic,* was enthusiastically received by the checker fraternity and many players have urged me to follow it up with another work of a similar nature. Therefore, during the past several years, I have been at work on *The Science of Checkers and Draughts,* a collection of end-game and mid-game studies by this writer, for the most part. However, a number of other authors have been included to round out the 101 selected situations that I hope will appeal to the student as well as the advanced player.

I consider the end-game the neglected art in checkers. Most students spend literally all of their time studying the openings and fail to appreciate the importance of end-game and mid-game study. This, of course, does not apply to all players, as the success of *Checker Magic* and the excellent works of Ben Boland will attest; but by and large the average player loses most of his games in the ending because of his failure to appreciate and understand this vital phase of scientific checkers.

Most of the positions shown in this book arose in actual play during my exhibitions, matches, team play, and New York knockout tourneys. A number of these settings have been composed, but are nevertheless instructive and valuable. If you think you can upset the terms of any of the problems shown, or can demonstrate a dual solution, you may send me your play and if it is sound you will receive credit in any future work that I may publish on the game.

I want to take this opportunity to thank the many thousands of checker players and enthusiasts who have read my books and have written me in appreciation. I hope that *The Science of Checkers and Draughts* will meet with your approval, too, and will be helpful to my readers in their study of the Grand Old Pastime.

T. W.

January 1972

Strategy and Tactics

Every player of checkers (and draughts, as it is often called), regardless of strength, must be concerned with strategy and tactics if he wishes to succeed as a player. Strategy is the art of deploying your forces in such a way as to defeat your opponent, or at least hold him to a draw. Tactics, on the other hand, involves the various methods of proceeding with the basic strategic plans and the adroit devices you can utilize along the way.

In my opinion, the greatest mistake the average player makes is trying to *win* every game. As a result he winds up losing nearly every game. My first piece of advice is, *keep the draw in sight*. In other words, do not play to win; rather play *not to lose*. This may sound like a negative approach, but it leads to affirmative results. The master always plays for the draw, except when he is playing the last game of a heat or match and is a game down. In that case, of course, a draw would be useless and hence he must go all out to win. But, as a rule, it is the soundest policy to play "safe" and let your opponent stick his neck out by trying for a win.

Another mistake that many players make is failing to take sufficient time before making a move. It may sound easy to obey the dictum *move slowly*, but it is one of the hardest rules to obey. After you have decided to make a move, instead of making it at once, *count to ten*; if you still want to make the move, go ahead, but if for any reason you think it might not be quite the best move, look the situation over more fully. This rule has saved many a game for me and I know you will find it useful.

As a student you need to be told that moves to the center of the board are nearly always better than moves to the side, since they have more power in the center, and squares 14 and 19 are key points of contention in many games. You also need to know that it is best to develop the men in your single corner (left-hand side) while retaining as much as possible the men in your double corner (right-hand side). Just remember that a player with a strong double corner is doubly hard to corner. When you are playing the Black side, try to keep your men on squares 1 and 3, for they form a bridge that makes it difficult for your opponent to get a king. Likewise, when you are handling the White pieces, try to keep your men stationed on squares 30 and 32. Many positions in this work revolve around a "bridge" position; Ben Boland, author of a fine book entitled *Boland's Bridges*, deals in it with this important phase of the game.

The art of the sacrifice is another aspect of the game covered in the following pages, and it is truly an art. Many students are loath to give up a man because they fear it may mean the loss of the game. Actually, it may mean the loss of the game if you do *not* sacrifice, or, what is just as bad, it could mean that you are allowing your opponent to escape what should be a win for you. While rather rare, there are even occasions when you will be able to sacrifice two men, or more, to gain your objective. Just bear in mind that position bests possession; so do not fear to give up a piece or two if you think the situation warrants such a sacrifice.

Just as there are "good" squares (14 and 19), so there are "bad" squares which you should try to avoid occupying— as a general rule. When you have Blacks, try to keep away from squares 21 and 28, the dog-holes. Likewise, when you have Whites, keep away from squares 12 and 5. Men on these squares have virtually no maneuverability and are almost like "zombies." True, there are exceptions to all these generalizations, and with experience and intuition you will learn to recognize them.

In chess, fast development is the order of the day. In checkers, however, slow development is preferred. In other words, try to keep your position intact as long as possible. The first player who is forced to break up his position is usually the one who loses. Such openings as 11-16, 23-19 and 12-16, 23-19 are actually barred, because the early break-up of White's game makes the position hopeless. The following maxim is well worth remembering in this regard: Moves that disturb your position the least disturb your opponent the most!

There are twelve men on each side of the board, but there is also a thirteenth man, the man behind the board! You must know this thirteenth man and study him as much as you study the men on the board. What are his weaknesses and what type of play will most likely be successful against him? Is he likely to "bite" on some bait, or is he too cautious? Is he a "book" player or a "crossboard" marvel? Learn as much as you can about your opponent before you sit down to play. Psychology plays a much larger role in checkers than the average player realizes, and every master makes the fullest use of his knowledge of his opponent when making his moves on the board.

Don't try to *win a drawn game*. I have seen many players, including experts, lose games that were only draws because they refused to give up what they fancied was an "advantage" in the ending. When the game is a certain draw, acknowledge it and go on to the next game. Once again, the exception is when you are a game down and playing the final game of the heat; you then have to play it for all it is worth without regard for the consequences.

Learn from your mistakes. Any player may lose a game in a certain fashion once, but try not to fall for the same shot or loss a second time. When you lose a game, go over it later and see where you made the losing move and resolve not to make that same mistake again. I have watched players lose the same exact game over and over again and often wonder if they are playing checkers or just "pushing wood." The games you lose can be of great value to you, *but you must learn from them and refuse to make the same mistake twice!*

Don't be afraid to play opponents who are stronger than yourself. In fact, you should make it a point to seek out, whenever you can, opponents who are superior, for that is the only way you are going to learn how to play scientific checkers. It may flatter your ego to play with someone you can beat every time, but it will not flatter your playing. Losing to a good player is much to be preferred to beating a weak player; while that is an obvious cliché, it is really surprising how many players refuse to abide by it.

Most books on checkers deal with the openings and comparatively very few with the end-game and mid-game. *The Science of Checkers and Draughts* is an attempt to make up for this deficiency. Few players devote as much attention to this phase of the game as they should and I strongly urge you to study the positions in this book so that you can improve your tactics and make use of all the tools at your command, once you have familiarized yourself with them.

Finally, if you can't be good, at least be fair. That is, play according to the rules at all times. In checkers, as in chess, you must play on the square.

In the following pages you will find a résumé of the standard laws of checkers. We urge you to learn them thoroughly and abide by them at all times, and insist that your opponent do likewise. If an opponent refuses to play "according to Hoyle," do not continue playing with him because it will surely affect your game—for the worse. Any good player is willing to abide by the rules, and you will find that most opponents will gladly accede to your wishes in this respect. Playing on the square is the only way to play the Game of Kings and the King of Games!

THE STANDARD LAWS OF CHECKERS AND DRAUGHTS

1. The Official Checker Board to be used in National Tournaments and Official Matches shall be of green and buff (or black and white, according to English rules) two-inch squares. The board shall be placed for playing so that the green double corners are on the right-hand side of the players. (NEVER the single-corner.)

2. The Official Checkers to be used in National Tournaments and Official Matches shall be turned and round, and red and white in color, and of a diameter of not less than one and one-quarter inches, or more than one and one-half inches. The pieces shall be placed on the green or black squares.

3. At the beginning of a contest the players shall toss for colors. The first move is made by the player having the red pieces (called Black in most textbooks). Thereafter, the players shall alternate in leading off with Red in each succeeding opening balloted.

4. At the end of five minutes (if the move has not already been made) "Time" must be called in a distinct manner by the person appointed for that purpose; and if the move is not completed *before* the end of another minute, the game shall be adjudged as lost through improper delay. When either player is deaf or partially deaf, a card on which the word "Time" is printed in large letters shall be placed or laid on the playing table when it is time to move.

5. When there are two or more ways to "jump," five minutes shall be allowed for the move. When there is only

one way to "jump," Time shall be called at the end of one minute; and if the move is not completed before the end of another minute the game shall be adjudged as lost through improper delay.

6. At the beginning of a game each player shall be entitled to arrange his own or his opponent's pieces properly on the squares. After the game has opened (a move has been made) if either player touch or arrange a piece without giving intimation, he shall be cautioned for the first offense, and shall forfeit the game for any subsequent offense of this kind. If a person, whose turn it is to play, touches one of his own playable pieces, he must either play it or forfeit the game. (In other words: play with your head, not with your hands.)

7. If any part of a playable piece be played over an angle of the square on which it is stationed, the play must be completed in that direction. Inadvertently removing, touching, or disturbing from its position a piece that is not playable, while in the act of jumping or making an intended move, does not constitute a move, and the piece or pieces shall be placed back in position and the game continued.

8. The "Huff" or "Blow" is hereby abolished. All jumps must be completed and all jumped pieces must be removed from the board. Note: This is probably one of the most controversial of all the rules. In many countries the huff still is law. (That is to say, when your opponent is negligent and overlooks a jump and improperly makes another move, he forfeits the game.) The late Willie Ryan, and many other masters, opposed the abolishment of the huff, since the present rule rewards, rather than punishes, poor playing.

9. When a single piece reaches the crownhead of the board, by reason of a move or as the completion of a jump,

it becomes a King; and that completes the move or jump. The piece must then be crowned by the opponent by placing a piece on top of it. If the opponent neglects to do so and makes a play, then any such play shall be put back until the piece that should have been crowned is crowned. "Time" does not start on the player whose piece should have been crowned until the piece is crowned. Note: This is one rule that many players refuse to obey; I never let my opponent move until he has given me a "hat."

10. A King once crowned can move in any direction, as the limits of the board permit. A King can jump in any direction one or more pieces, as the limits of the board permit. When a piece is not available for crowning, one must be furnished by the Referee. Note: Nine men *can* be jumped at one time, but don't expect to see it soon.

11. A Draw is declared when neither player can force a win. When one side appears stronger than the other, and the player with what appears to be the weaker side requests the Referee for a Count on Moves, then, if the Referee so decides, the stronger party is required to complete the win, or show to the satisfaction of the Referee at least an "increased" advantage over his opponent within forty of his own moves, these to be counted from the point at which notice was given by the Referee, failing in which he must relinquish the game as a draw. Note: For some reason this rule is often misunderstood. However, any competent Referee should have no trouble in enforcing the "spirit" of the law.

12. After an opening is balloted, neither player shall leave the board without permission of the Referee. If permission is granted, his opponent may accompany him, or the Referee may designate a person to accompany him. "Time" shall be deducted accordingly from the player whose turn it is to move. Note: In chess, games are often "adjourned"

for days at a time, with both players having plenty of opportunity to examine the position—either alone or with others. This is one rule most checker players have never been able to understand or appreciate.

13. Anything that may tend to either annoy or distract the attention of an opponent is strictly forbidden, such as making signs or sounds, pointing or hovering over the board with either the hands or the head, or unnecessarily delaying to move a piece touched. (Note: Good moves by your opponent cannot be considered an "annoyance," even though they may bother you.) Any principal so acting, after having been warned of the consequences by the Referee and requested to desist, shall forfeit the game.

14. Players shall be allowed to smoke during a game, but care must be exercised not to blow smoke across the board, lest it annoy an opponent. If a player is thus annoyed, he may object to his opponent's smoking, in which case neither player shall be allowed to smoke. Note: Pipes and cigars have been known to wilt many an opponent.

15. Any spectator giving warning, either by signs or sound or remark, in any of the games, whether playing or pending, shall be ordered from the room during the contest. Play shall be discontinued until such offending party retires. Spectators shall not be allowed to smoke or talk near the playing boards.

Note: These rules, by and large, have been in existence for over a century and were originally drafted by Andrew Anderson, World Champion, in 1852. With one or two exceptions they have served their purpose well. The notable exceptions are the time-limit rule and the huff. I would very much like to see reforms enacted in these two cases. (T.W.)

Composers (Other than Tom Wiswell) Who Have Contributed to This Book

CLAYTON BEEBE

BEN BOLAND

DR. T. J. BROWN

JOHN CARY

HAROLD FREYER

ARTHUR GLADSTONE

A. W. GLASSON

C. J. GREENSWORD

E. A. HARBER

MILTON JOHNSON

GEORGE L. KING

JULES LEOPOLD

CHRIS NELSON

DEREK OLDBURY

HOWARD PECK

ANTHONY PETRONELLA

S. J. PICKERING

JIMMY RICCA

BILLY SALOT

DR. AUGUST SCHAEFER

HERMAN SCHECTER

DR. LEWIS SCHREIBER

PAUL SEMPLE

JOHN SMARRA

AL SPRANGLE

HENRY TODER

ALBERT N. WHITE

JAMES WYLLIE

and

AUTHOR UNKNOWN

My sincere thanks to all the above players for their cooperation in helping make this work possible.   T. W.

THE
SCIENCE
OF
CHECKERS AND DRAUGHTS

BY THE NUMBERS

If you are a beginner or a student of checkers, I urge you to study the numbered board shown below, and become familiar with the "language of the checkerboard." In actual play the darker squares are used, but in books and magazines we employ the light squares, purely for the sake of clarity.

THE NUMBERED BOARD
(BLACK)

(WHITE)

Place the Black men on squares 1 to 12, and the White men on squares 21 to 32 at the start of each game.

The solutions to the problems are given below the positions, and are read across the page. I suggest that you cover the solution with a blotter or your hand and try to solve the problems without looking at the answers. In that way you will get the most benefit and, indeed, the most pleasure and satisfaction. The notes given below help explain the various points and should be studied with care. Most, but not all, positions show White to play. Do not attach any significance to the numbers; they are only a means of communication between author and reader. Good moving and good luck!

101 End-game and Mid-game Problems

THE LITTLE FOOLER

(BLACK)

(WHITE)

PROBLEM NUMBER 1
By Tom Wiswell and Jimmy
Ricca
BLACK: 5 KING 3
WHITE: 30 KING 22
TERMS: White to play and
win

SOLUTION

22–17!——A, 3-7——B, 17-14, 7-11, 14-10, 11-16 (5-9, 30-26), 10-15, 5-9——C, 30-26, 9-14, 26-22, 14-18, 15-11 ——D, 18-25 (16-7, 22-15), 11-20, 25-30, 20-24, 30-26, 24-27——E, White wins.

A——If 22-18, 5-9, 18-15, 3-8, 15-10 (30-26, 9-14), 9-13, 10-15, 8-12, 15-11, 13-17, 11-15, 12-16, 15-18, 16-20, drawn. White can play otherwise but Black draws against all lines of this variation.

B——If 5-9, 17-13, 9-14, 13-9, 14-17, 9-14, 17-21, 14-10, White wins.

C——It's "now or never."

D——The *coup de grace!* Note that this exchange does *not* change "the move," because neither capturing piece is removed from the board.

E——Termed "a fine original problem" by the celebrated Ben Boland, Dean of Problem Editors.

CHANGING GUARD

(BLACK)

(WHITE)

PROBLEM NUMBER 2
By Dr. T. J. Brown
BLACK: 1   KING 3
WHITE: 31   KING 11
TERMS: White to play and win

SOLUTION

31–26——A, 1-6, 26-22——B, 6-9 (6-10, 22-17), 22-18
——C, 9-13, 18-15, 13-17, 11-16——D, 3-8, 16-12——E,
8-3, 15-11——F, 17-22, 12-16——F, 22-26, 16-19, 26-31,
19-23—G, White wins.

A——Necessary; if 31-27, 1-6, 27-23, 6-10, 23-19, 10-14,
etc., drawn.

B——Again the only move to win for White.

C——Of course, if 22-17, 9-13, 17-14, 13-17, etc., drawn.

D——Watch the "changing of the guard" take place, a basic
winning idea.

E——Forcing the King back and allowing the single man to
"switch" places with the White King.

F——A useful theme that should win many games for you in
the future.

G——The study of many "simple" ideas like this will make
you a finer end-game player—and that is where most players fall down: in the final stages of the game.

MINORITY RULE

(BLACK)

(WHITE)

PROBLEM NUMBER 3
By Tom Wiswell
BLACK: 5, 9, 13
WHITE: KINGS 3, 18
TERMS: White to play and win

SOLUTION

18–23——A, 9-14——B, 3-7, 5-9——C (13-17, 7-10), 7-10, 14-17, 10-15——D, 17-21——E (9-14, 15-18), 23-18, 9-14——F, 18-9, 13-17, 15-18, 21-25, 9-14, 17-22——G, 14-10, 25-29, 18-25, 29-22, 10-14——H, White wins.

A——"Going away," and the right square from which to force the win.

B——If 13-17, 3-7, 17-21 (or 22), 7-10, etc., White wins.

C——If 14-17, 7-10, 17-21, 10-14, 13-17, 23-26, etc., White wins.

D——NOT 23-18, 17-22, 18-25, 9-14, and Black wins!

E——If 17-22, 23-18, etc., White wins.

F——Of course, 13-17 or 21-25 lose by 18-14, etc.

G——If 17-21, 18-22, 25-29, 22-26, 29-25, 15-18, etc., White wins.

H——My lone win in a six game encounter with former Connecticut State Champion, Howard Peck, played June 21, 1969 (the opening was 10-15, 22-17, 6-10). The win was highly praised by the late A. J. Mantell, the noted critic and analyst.

GRAND MASTER

(BLACK)

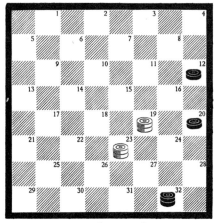

(WHITE)

PROBLEM NUMBER 4
By James Wyllie
BLACK: 12, 20 KING 32
WHITE: KINGS 19, 23
TERMS: White to play and draw

SOLUTION

23–26, 32-28, 26-31, 20-24, 19-23, 12-16, 31-26——A, 28-32, 26-31, 16-20, 31-26, 24-27, 26-31, 20-24, 31-26——B, 27-31, 26-22, 31-27, 22-18, 27-31, 18-22, 24-28, 22-18, 31-27, 23-19, 27-24, 19-23, 24-20, 18-22, 20-16, 22-18, 16-11, 18-14——C, 11-15, 14-9, 15-10, 9-5——D, drawn.

A——If 23-27, 16-19, 27-20, 19-23, Black wins.

B——If 23-19, 32-28, 19-23, 27-32, 31-26, 24-27, Black wins.

C——Note that if 18-22, 11-15, 22-26, 15-10, 26-22, 10-14, 22-26, 14-17, 26-31, 17-22, 23-26, 22-18, 26-23, 18-27, 31-24, 32-27, 24-31, 28-32, Black wins.

D—A gem from yesteryear; we did not think it appropriate to publish a book on end-games without an example of the genius and craftmanship of the great Wyllie, champion of the world for forty years! Along with Dr. Marion Tinsley, Richard Jordan, Samuel Gonotsky and James Ferrie, Wyllie was one of the "greatest of the great!"

THE DODGER

(BLACK)

(WHITE)

PROBLEM NUMBER 5
By Tom Wiswell

BLACK: 23 KINGS 16, 17
WHITE: 20 KINGS 11, 32
TERMS: White to play and win

SOLUTION

11–15, 16-12, 15-18, 23-26, 18-22, 17-14——A, 22-31, 14-10, 32-27——B, 10-15, 27-23——C, 15-11, 23-19, 12-8——D, 20-16——E, 11-20, 19-24, 20-27, 31-24, 8-11, 24-19——F, White wins.

A——Black hopes to gain square 11 and avoid defeat via "Payne's Draw"; the irony of it is that he gets to square 11 —but still loses.

B——White's strategy is worth noting as this position is from actual play and may well win a game for you in the future.

C——Not 27-24, 12-8, etc., drawn.

D——Black would seem to be free—but wait a minute!

E——An old "dodge": it prevents "Payne's Draw" by getting "the move" on the remaining King. If 19-16, 11-7, draws, and if 31-27, 8-3, draws.

F——From the finals of a New York Knockout Tourney won by the writer on December 3, 1968.

SANCTUARY

PROBLEM NUMBER 6
By Tom Wiswell
BLACK: 1, 6 KING 22
WHITE: 5, 23 KING 21
TERMS: White to play and
draw

SOLUTION

23–19——A, 6-10, 19-16——A, 10-15, 16-11, 15-19, 11-7,
19-23——B, 7-3, 23-26, 3-7 (not 3-8), 26-31, 7-10——C,
22-18——D, 10-7, 18-14, 7-11, 31-27, 11-15, 27-24, 21-25
——E, 14-17——F, 15-10, 24-19, 25-21, 17-22, 10-14——
G, etc., drawn.

A——Black has "the move" and threatens to "corner" the
second White King.

B——Allowing Black to crown on square 30, 31, or 32; it is
usually wise to make the move that allows the most freedom
of movement.

C——Now White must make some "key" moves to maintain
the draw.

D——Necessary, to prevent 10-14 and the "sanctuary" of
14-9, etc.

E——NOW White can make this move, in fact, must make it
to draw.

F——Nothing better; if 24-20 White must avoid 15-19, 14-
18, Black wins.

32

G——White finally gains the safety of a snug harbor.

MASTERPIECE

(BLACK)

(WHITE)

PROBLEM NUMBER 7
By "Unknown"
BLACK: 7, 20 KING 19
WHITE: 27 KINGS 8, 32
TERMS: White to play and
win

SOLUTION

8–3, 7-10——A, 3-7, 10-14, 7-10, 14-17, 10-14, 17-21, 14-18, 19-24——B, 27-23, 24-27——C, 32-28, 27-32 (21-25, 18-22), 18-22, 32-27, 23-18, 27-32 (27-23, 22-17), 18-14, 32-27, 14-10, 27-23, 10-7, 23-19, 22-26——D, 21-25, 26-30, 25-29, 7-3, 20-24, 3-7, 24-27, 28-32——E, 27-31, 7-11, 19-23, 11-15, 31-26, 15-19, 23-16, 30-23, 29-25, 32-27, 25-22, 27-24——F, White wins.

A——If 7-11, 3-8, 11-15, 8-11, 15-18, 11-15, 19-10, 27-24, White wins.

B——If 21-25, 18-23, 19-26, 27-24, 20-27, 32-21, White wins.

C——If 21-25, 32-28, 24-27, 18-15, 27-18, 22-15, 25-30, 15-19, White wins.

D——A beautiful move; now, if 20-24, 26-31, etc., White wins.

E—White allows Black to get three Kings and still wins, a most remarkable position and worthy of your close study.

F——Every move has a meaning all its own. I regret that **33** we do not know the author of this pure gem. If you know, please communicate with me so that I can supply his name in the next edition.

THE DECK HAND

(BLACK)

(WHITE)

PROBLEM NUMBER 8
By Chris Nelson
BLACK: 12, 20 KING 21
WHITE: 6 KINGS 11, 22
TERMS: White to play and
win

SOLUTION

11–15, 12-16——A, 15-11, 16-19, 11-16, 19-24, 16-19, 24-28, 6-2, 28-32, 2-7, 32-28, 7-10, 20-24, 22-26, 24-27, 26-31, 27-32, 10-14, 21-25, 14-17, 25-30, 17-21——B, White wins.
A——If 20-24, 15-19, White wins.
B——The cover problem for November 1930, of *The Draughts Review.*

Here is another fine problem by the celebrated Mr. Nelson:
BLACK: 16 KINGS 4, 30
WHITE: KINGS 3, 22, 23
TERMS: White to play and win

SOLUTION

23–27, 16-20, 22-18, 30-26, 18-15, 26-22, 3-7, 22-17, 7-10, 17-13, 10-14, 4-8, 27-32, 8-3, 15-11, 20-24, 11-15, 3-7, 15-19, White wins. Chris, a former longshoreman, was known to all as "The Deck Hand."

CONFRONTATION

(BLACK)

(WHITE)

PROBLEM NUMBER 9
By Herman Schecter
BLACK: 5, 14, 27
WHITE: 9, 30 KING 15
TERMS: White to play and win

SOLUTION

9–6, 27-31, 6-2, 31-27, 15-10!——A, 14-18 (14-17, 10-14), 30-26!——B, 27-31——C, 2-6, 31-22, 6-9, 5-14, 10-26—— D, White wins.

A——A beautiful move that wins neatly and decisively; if 2-6, 27-23, 6-9, 14-17, 9-14 (15-18, 5-14, 18-27, 14-18, drawn), 17-22, 15-18, 5-9, 18-27, 9-18, etc., drawn.

B——Completes the "one-two punch" started with 15-10 and delivers the knock-out punch that wins the fight.

C——Otherwise 10-15 wins for White.

D——Herman Schecter is one of New York's "top ten" and has good scores with the leading New York Masters. He is a "crossboard" player on the order of Kenneth Grover and Morris Krantz and is always a dangerous opponent. It is a pleasure to include one of his fine end-game studies in this collection.

EARLY AMERICAN

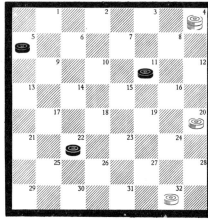

(BLACK)

(WHITE)

PROBLEM NUMBER 10
By A. Schaefer
BLACK: 5, 11, 22
WHITE: 20, 32 KING 4
TERMS: White to play and win

SOLUTION

4–8, 11-15, 8-11, 15-18——A, 11-15, 5-9, 32-27——B, 9-13, 20-16, 13-17, 16-11——C, 17-21, 11-7——C, 21-25, 7-2——C, 25-30, 2-6——C, 30-26, 6-9——C, 26-31, 9-13——D, 31-24, 13-17——D, 24-19, 15-24, 22-26, 17-14——E, 18-22, 24-27, 26-30, 27-23, 22-25, 14-17, 25-29, 17-21, 29-25, 23-18, White wins.

A——Of course, if 15-19, 11-15, 19-24, 15-18, 22-25, 18-22, etc., White wins.

B——Sooner or later, this is a necessary move.

C——These are all star moves, essential to the win, as you will see.

D——This is why the above moves were all necessary to the final win.

E——Into the "American Position," where White has "the move" and forces the enemy forces into the single corner for a "standard" win.

THE RETREAT

(BLACK)

(WHITE)

PROBLEM NUMBER 11
By Ben Boland and Tom Wiswell
BLACK: 7, 23, 28
WHITE: 24, 32 KING 6
TERMS: White to play and win

SOLUTION

24–19——A, 23-26, 19-16, 26-31, 16-12, 31-26, 12-8, 26-23, 8-3, 7-11, 6-10, 23-19, 3-8, 11-16, 8-11, 16-20, 11-8 (The Retreat) 19-23, 10-15, 20-24, 8-12, 24-27, 15-19, 23-16, 12-19, 27-31, 19-15——B, White wins.

A——6-2 allows a draw as in the following setting by the writer:

BLACK: 1, 6 KING 27
WHITE: 5, 18, 23, 32
TERMS: White to play and draw

SOLUTION

32-28, 6-9 (6-10, 23-19, 27-24, 19-16, 24-27, 16-11, 27-23, 28-24, etc., draws) 28-24, 27-20, 23-19, 20-24, 19-15, 24-19, 15-10, 19-23, 18-15, 23-18, 15-11, 18-15, 11-7, 15-6, 7-2, drawn. A basic theme that is more often than not overlooked by the student—and, sometimes, the expert.

B——The celebrated Ben Boland is the author of such best-sellers as: *Famous Positions, Boland's Bridges, Masterpieces,* and *Familiar Themes* and is always at work on still another book of end-games. He is a walking encyclopedia on problems and themes and his works are a history of The Problem.

SURPRISE PARTY

(BLACK)

(WHITE)

PROBLEM NUMBER 12
By John Smarra
BLACK: 24 KINGS 1, 4
WHITE: 5, 9, 16, 32
TERMS: White to play and win

SOLUTION

16–12——A, 24-28, 9-6!!——B, 1-10, 5-1, 10-15——C, 1-6, 15-19, 6-10, 19-16, 10-7, 16-20, 7-11, 20-24, 12-8, 24-19, 8-3, 19-24, 3-7, 24-19, 7-10, 19-24, 10-15, 24-20, 15-18, 20-24, 18-22——D, etc., White wins.

A——16-11 and 32-28 allow draws, as a little study will show.

B——The only move to win and the surprise move that many solvers overlook. Although the technique involved is quite simple (having "the move"), it is an idea that just does not occur to many players until they have exhausted all the other possibilities—and sometimes not even then.

C——If 10-7, 1-6, 7-3, 6-10, 4-8, 10-15, 8-11, 15-8, 3-7, 32-27, White wins.

D——A fine example of this composer's work. John is a young New York expert with a flair for the original and unexpected in his compositions and endings. He received much of his inspiration from *Let's Play Checkers*, by the writer and Ken Grover, so I must say that I am very pleased with his development.

38

HAPPINESS IS—WINNING

(BLACK)

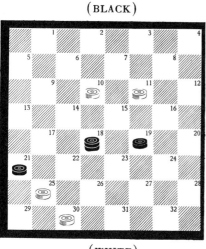

(WHITE)

PROBLEM NUMBER 13
By Milton Johnson
BLACK: 19, 21 KING 18
WHITE: 10, 11, 25, 30
TERMS: White to play and win

SOLUTION

11–7, 19-23, 7-2——A, 23-27, 10-6, 27-31, 6-1, 31-27, 2-6, 18-23, 1-5, 23-26, 30-23, 27-18, 6-10, 21-30, 10-14, 18-9, 5-14——B, White wins.

A——If 10-6, 18-15, 7-2, 23-26, 30-23, 21-30, etc. drawn.

B——A good example of the skill of the noted Milton Johnson, former pride of Chicago, now a retired Floridian. Many of his fine end-games and compositions have appeared in the Checker Press, both here and abroad. Here is an early brain-child of Milton's that still casts a glow:

> BLACK: 11, 24 KINGS 4, 32
> WHITE: 7, 10, 23, 31
> TERMS: Black to play and win
> ### SOLUTION
> 32-27, 23-18, 27-23, 18-14, 23-18, 14-9, 18-15, 9-6, 24-27, 31-24, 15-19, 24-8, 4-9, Black wins.

TIME-BOMB

(BLACK)

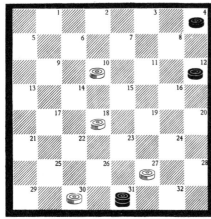

(WHITE)

PROBLEM NUMBER 14
By C. J. Greensword
BLACK: 4, 12 KING 31
WHITE: 10, 18, 27, 30
TERMS: White to play and win

SOLUTION

27–24——A, 31-27, 24-20, 27-23, 18-14, 23-18, 14-9, 18-14, 10-6, 14-5, 6-2, 5-9——B, 2-7, 9-14, 7-11, 14-18, 30-26——C, 12-16, 26-23!, 18-27, 11-15——D, etc., White wins.

A——White must return the piece, but when? The timing is always important and, in this case, leads to an instructive and entertaining finish.

B——If 4-8, 2-6, 8-11, 6-10, etc., White wins.

C——The start of a pretty combination that will please and instruct.

D——Because after the jump (20-11) White has "the move" and wins via *first position*. A good example of the genius of this famous English problemist who published hundreds of fine end-games.

AUTHOR! AUTHOR!

(BLACK)

(WHITE)

PROBLEM NUMBER 15
By Arthur Gladstone
BLACK: 7 KINGS 20, 22
WHITE: 15, 19, 27 KING 4
TERMS: White to play and win

SOLUTION

27–23, 20-24, 23-18——A, B, 22-17, 19-16, 24-20, 15-11, 7-10, 18-14, 10-15, 14-10, 17-14, 11-8——C, 20-11, 8-3, 14-7, 3-19——H, White wins.

A——If 15-11, 7-16, 19-12, 24-27, 23-19, 27-24, 19-15, 24-19, 15-10, 19-15, 10-7, 15-11, 7-2, 22-18, 12-8, 18-15, 8-3, 15-10, 3-8, 10-15, 8-12, 15-10, 12-8, 10-15, 2-6, 11-7, drawn.

B——19-16, 24-20, 16-12, 20-24, 4-8——D, E, F, 7-11, 23-18——G, 24-20, 8-3, 20-16, 15-8, 22-15, 8-4, 16-11, drawn.

C——If the man on square 10 crowns square 1, 2, or 3, the position is a draw.

D——12-8, 7-11, 15-10, 11-16, 8-3, 24-27, etc., drawn.

E——If 23-19, 7-11——G, 15-8, 24-15, 8-3, 15-11, 3-8, 11-16, drawn.

F——If 23-18, 24-19, 15-11, drawn.

G——22-18, 12-8, 18-11, 8-3, 24-15, 3-19, White wins.

H——Arthur Glatstein, of The Scorpion Club fame, is also Arthur Gladstone, the New York star.

KILLING TIME
(And your opponent)

(BLACK)

(WHITE)

PROBLEM NUMBER 16
By Tom Wiswell
BLACK: 11, 16, 19, 28
WHITE: 27, 32 KING 30
TERMS: White to play and win

SOLUTION

30–26——A, 11-15——B, 27-23——C, 19-24, 26-31——D, 16-20——E, 31-26——D, 24-27, 26-31——F, 20-24, 23-19——G, White wins.

A——Although White is one down, he has "position" and forces the win with "delaying" tactics that are instructive.

B——If 19-24, 27-20, 16-19, 26-22, 19-23 (11-15, 22-26), 22-18, 23-26, 32-27, etc., and the man on square 11 cannot be saved.

C——If 26-22 (or 26-31), 16-20, 22-26, 15-18, etc., draws.

D——White just "kills time," and this kills Black in the process!

E——If 15-19, 31-26, 24-27, 26-22, 19-26, 22-24, White wins.

F——White finally outwaits and outwits Black for an unusual win.

G——Embarrassing moments!

42

CHECKER CHARADE

(BLACK)

(WHITE)

PROBLEM NUMBER 17

By Jules Leopold

BLACK: 13 KINGS 10, 22

WHITE: 17, 32 KINGS 16, 30

TERMS: White to play and win

SOLUTION

16–19, 22-18, 19-23, 18-27, 32-23, 13-22, 23-18——A, 10-6, 18-14, 6-1, 14-9, 1-5, 9-6, 5-9, 6-1, 9-14, 1-6, 14-18, 6-10, 18-23, 10-15, 22-26——B, 15-19——C, 23-16, 30-23——D, White wins.

A——The White piece, with "the move," is stronger than the King, because of its "potential" power and maneuverability.

B——If 23-18, 30-25, 18-11, 25-18, White wins.

C——The unkindest cut of all.

D——The author, Jules Leopold, is a strong New York player and was a member of the New York Team that journeyed to Belfast in May 1968 to battle there for the International Team title. Although the owner of a large library on the game, he is strictly a "crossboard" player and, like the late "Sunset" Bell, enjoys playing for strokes and traps—often with success.

THE RIGHT MOMENT

(BLACK)

(WHITE)

PROBLEM NUMBER 18
By Tom Wiswell
BLACK: 1, 2, 24 KING 8
WHITE: 9, 10, 13, 23
TERMS: Black to play and
win

SOLUTION

24–27——A, 9-6——B, 2-9, 13-6, 27-31, 6-2, 31-26, 23-18, 26-22, 18-14, 22-17, 14-9——C, 17-13!, 10-7, 13-6, 2-9, 1-6, 9-2, 8-3——D, Black wins.

A——Note how the Black King remains at his post all through the maneuvering, waiting for the right moment to deliver the fatal blow.

B——This must be done sooner or later and 23-18 does not change the ultimate result.

C——If 2-6, 17-13, 6-2, 8-3, Black wins.

D——At last the Black King comes into the picture! Had Black varied from the above, the result would have been a draw instead of a win. From an actual game played at our favorite meeting place: The Chess and Checker Club of New York, probably the largest club of its kind in the nation.

BLACK AND WHITE

(BLACK)

(WHITE)

PROBLEM NUMBER 19
By Albert N. White
BLACK: 1, 3, 14, 25
WHITE: 12, 20, 21 KING 2
TERMS: Black to play and win

SOLUTION

25–30, 20-16, 30-26, 16-11——A, 26-31——B, 11-8——C, 31-26, 8-4, 26-22, 4-8, 22-17, 8-11, 17-13, 11-15, 13-9, 15-19, 14-18, 19-15, 18-22 (necessary), 15-18——D, 22-25, 21-17——E, 9-13, 17-14, 1-6, 2-9, 13-6, 18-22, 25-30, 22-17, 30-26, 17-13, 6-1, 14-9, 1-5, 9-6, 5-1, 6-2, 26-22, 13-9, 22-18, 9-5, 18-14——F, Black wins.

A——Forms Problem No. 1030 in Gould's *Problem Book* with this continuation: 14-18, 21-17, 26-22, 17-14, 22-17, 14-10 (2-7 draws), 17-13, etc., drawn.

B——Corrects 14-18, by W. J. Wray, *Gould's Problems*, page 357.

C——If 11-7, 3-10, 2-6, 10-15, 6-10, 14-18, 10-19, 18-23, 19-26, 31-22, 12-8, 1-6, 8-3, 6-9, 3-7, 22-18, Black wins.

D——15-10, 22-26, 21-17, 9-13, 17-14, 26-30, 10-15, 1-6, 2-9, 13-6, Black wins.

E——18-22, 25-29, 22-18, 29-25, 18-15, 1-6, 15-19, 9-5, 2-9, 5-14, Black wins.

F——Albert N. White is the Rochester, New York expert who once defeated Newell Banks in a National Championship Tourney. This is a fine correction of W. J. Wray, a great problemist.

THE CLINCHER

(BLACK)

(WHITE)

PROBLEM NUMBER 20
By Bill Salot
BLACK: 2, 6, 15, 18
WHITE: 24, 28, 30, 31
TERMS: White to play and win

SOLUTION

24–20, 18-23——A, 20-16, 2-7——A, 16-12, 7-11, 12-8, 11-16, 8-3, 16-20, 3-7, 15-18, 7-2, 6-9, 2-6, 9-13, 31-26——B, 23-27, 6-10, 27-31, 10-15, 31-22, 30-25, 22-29, 15-22——C, White wins.

A——These are the best moves at Black's disposal; other moves may be tried but they all end up in a blind alley. White forces his plan in fine style.

B——The pretty "clincher" that leads to the beautiful "Spread Eagle" theme once again. New themes are few and far between but original settings, such as this, are well worthy of production as they reveal the imagination and inspiration of the true composer.

C——Mr. Salot has many fine problems in print and I consider this a good example of his skill. He is also a fine crossboard player and occasionally visits the New York Club, where he holds his own with the best of them.

A GEM OF SEMPLECITY

(BLACK)

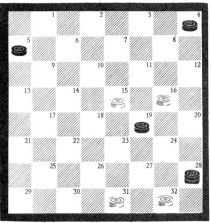

(WHITE)

PROBLEM NUMBER 21
By Paul Semple
BLACK: 4, 5, 19 KING 28
WHITE: 15, 16, 31, 32
TERMS: White to play and win

SOLUTION

31-27——A, 5-9, 16-11, 9-14, 15-10, 14-18, 10-7, 18-22——B, 7-2, 22-26, 27-23, 19-24, 23-19, 26-30, 2-7, 30-26, 11-8, 4-11, 7-16——C, 24-27——D, 32-23, 28-24, 16-20, 24-15, 23-19, 15-24, 20-27——E, White wins.

A——Effectively negating the power of the Black King and forcing all the play from here to the brilliant finish.

B——If 19-23, 7-2, 23-26, 2-7, and Black cannot escape the shot via 27-24, 28-19, 11-8, etc., Black wins.

C——Threatening the man on square 24 and forcing the sacrifice.

D——It appears that Black has a draw, but we really have a Semple win!

E——The late Paul Semple, of Martins Ferry, Ohio, was a checker magician and a semi-professional magician, giving shows on weekends in various Ohio towns. His magic on the board was revealed in many fine problems like the one above.

BRIDGE TO VICTORY

(BLACK)

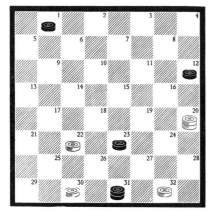

(WHITE)

PROBLEM NUMBER 22
By Tom Wiswell
BLACK: 1, 12, 23 KING 31
WHITE: 22, 30, 32 KING 20
TERMS: White to play and win

SOLUTION

22–18——A, 31-27——B, 18-15, 1-6, 15-11, 6-10, 11-7, 10-14, 7-2, 14-17, 2-6, 17-22, 6-10, 22-26, 10-15, 26-31, 30-25!——C, White wins.

A——Of course, if White plays 20-24 then 23-26, 30-23, 31-26, etc., drawn without any difficulty.

B——Otherwise White can win with 20-24, etc., for Black cannot withstand the attack of the two White Kings in the offing.

C——This quiet move completely ties up all the Black forces and compels "unconditional surrender." Another instructive ending from actual play. Many instructive "bridge" endings may be found in that excellent work, *Boland's Bridges*, by Brooklyn's brilliant Ben Boland, and we recommend it to duffer and expert alike. He is also the author of *Masterpieces in the Game of Checkers*, *Border Classics*, and *Famous Positions*, all landmarks in checker literature.

GLASSON'S GEM

(BLACK)

(WHITE)

PROBLEM NUMBER 23

By A. W. Glasson

BLACK: 12, 18, 24 KING 22
WHITE: 20, 31 KINGS 2, 15
TERMS: White to play and win

SOLUTION

15-19——A, 24-28, 20-16——B, 28-32, 2-7, 32-28, 7-10——C, 28-24, 19-28, 12-19, 10-15, 19-23, 15-19, 23-26, *31-27!!!*——D, 26-31——E, 19-15, 31-24, 28-19——F, White wins.

A——Because if 2-6 or 2-7 Black can draw with 22-26, 31-22, 18-25, etc. With this move (15-19) White initiates a fine attack that culminates in a beautiful surprise move near the finish.

B——This move immobilizes Black and forces matters from here on.

C——NOT 31-27, 22-17, 19-15, 12-19, 15-13, 28-32, drawn.

D——A stunning play that wins just when it appears that Black will escape.

E——Of course, if 18-23, White wins on "the move," and if 26-30, 19-23, White wins, etc.

F——A fine example of the artistry of Mr. Glasson, of Cornwall, England, it originally appeared in *The English Draughts Journal* in 1967.

THE LONG, LONG TRAIL

(BLACK)

(WHITE)

PROBLEM NUMBER 24
By Author Unknown
BLACK: 2, 21, 28 KING 4
WHITE: 11, 19, 30, 32
TERMS: White to play and win

SOLUTION

19–16, 2-6, 16-12, 6-10, 11-7, 10-14, 7-2, 14-17, 2-7, 17-22, 7-11, 22-25, 11-15, 25-29, 15-18, 29-25, 32-27, 28-32, 27-24, 32-27, 24-19, 27-24, 19-15, 24-19, 15-10, 19-16, 10-7, 16-11, 7-2, 11-16, 2-7, 16-19, 7-10, 19-16, 10-14, 16-11, 14-17, 11-7, 17-22, 25-29, 18-14, 7-11, 14-10, 11-16, 10-7, 16-19, 7-11, 19-23, 12-8, 23-19, 8-3, 19-23, 3-8, 23-19, 8-12, 19-24, 12-16, 24-27, 16-20, 27-32, 20-24, 32-28, 24-27, 28-32, 22-26, 32-23, 26-19, 29-25, 30-26, 25-29, 19-15, 21-25, 15-19, 25-30, 11-16, 30-23, 19-26——A, White wins.

A——The longest, if not the most difficult, problem in the book. Many of the moves are necessary, otherwise Black can escape. I do not know the author of this very fine position, which was sent to James Garrison by J. H. Armitage, and originally appeared in the January 1959 issue of the *California Checker Chatter*, Leonard Hall's fine magazine on the West Coast.

TOM, JULES, AND JACK

(BLACK)

(WHITE)

PROBLEM NUMBER 25
By Tom Wiswell
BLACK: 7, 10, 12, 18
WHITE: 14, 19, 20, 30
TERMS: White to play and draw

SOLUTION

14–9, 7-11, 9-6, 11-15, 19-16 (necessary) 12-19, 6-2, 10-14, 2-7, 14-17——A, 20-16——B, 17-21——C, 16-12, 19-24 ——D, 12-8, 15-19, 7-11, 18-23, 11-16——E, 24-28, 16-20, 28-32, 20-16, 32-28, 16-20, 23-27, 20-24, 19-23, 24-31, 23-27, 31-24, 28-19——F, drawn.

A——Here is one neat draw against 18-22: 18-22, 7-10, 14-18, 10-14, 19-23, 20-16 (if 14-10, 22-26, etc., Black wins), 15-19 (22-26, 14-10, now draws), 14-17, 22-26, 30-25, 19-24, 17-22, etc., draws.

B——The White King stands as a watchman to see which way the enemy decides to flee; at the same time he is getting a second King.

C——If 17-22, 12-8, 19-23, 7-10, drawn.

D——If 18-22, 7-11, 15-18, 11-15, 19-24, 15-19, 24-28, 12-8, etc., drawn.

E——Necessary, as 8-3 allows a Black win, while this is a cleancut draw.

F——From some analysis of a game played between the writer and Jules Leopold and Jack Botte, in tandem (10-24-68).

MATCH POINT

(BLACK)

(WHITE)

PROBLEM NUMBER 26
By Tom Wiswell
BLACK: 2, 8 KINGS 24, 25
WHITE: 10, 15, 22, 32
        KING 9
TERMS: White to play and
        win

SOLUTION

15–11——A, 8-15, 10-6, 25-18, 32-28!——B, 24-20, 28-24, 20-27, 9-5, 2-9, 5-32——C, White wins.

A——The only move to win, if 22-17, or 22-18, 24-19, etc., draws. For example: 22-17, 24-19, 9-5, 25-22, 17-13, 22-26 (NOT 22-18), 13-9, 26-23, 9-6, 2-9, 5-14, 8-12, etc., draws. This was the last of a four-game match I was playing and I needed a win to clinch the heat, and so I got particular pleasure when I spied the neat victory ahead.

B——Black is one man up but will soon be one game down, a comment I may have made elsewhere, but a very appropriate description of this type of situation. Always be on the lookout for these sacrifices; they are the type of maneuver most players tend to overlook in the heat of battle—and are pointed out by the "kibitzers" later.

C——From 11-16, 24-19, 7-11, a difficult three-mover. I prefer to have the weak side first in these heats, so I can go "all out" with White.

THE CHEERFUL GIVER

(BLACK)

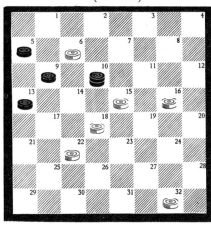

(WHITE)

PROBLEM NUMBER 27
By Tom Wiswell
BLACK: 5, 9, 13 KING 10
WHITE: 6, 15, 16, 18, 22, 32
TERMS: White to play and win

SOLUTION

15–11——A, 10-1, 32-28——B, 1-6——C, 28-24——D, 6-10——C, 24-19, 10-14——C, 11-7——E, 14-23, 16-11 ——E, 23-16, 7-3——E, 16-7, 3-10——F, White wins.

A——White's only move to win.

B——Or 32-27.

C——Being a man down, Black's moves are virtually dictated from here to the end, but White must reply correctly to make the most of the ending.

D——Of course, if 18-15, Black replies with 13-17 and against anything else (except 28-24) 6-10 lets Black slip away.

E——White's generosity is exceeded only by his resourcefulness; these "give-away" themes are frequently overlooked by the student—and by some players who are no longer students.

F——Continue: 9-14, 10-17, 5-9, 17-21, 9-14, 21-25, etc., White wins. The Lord loveth a "cheerful giver"!

IDIOT'S DELIGHT

(BLACK)

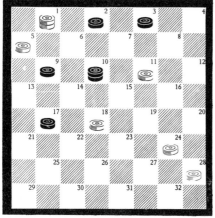

(WHITE)

PROBLEM NUMBER 28
By Tom Wiswell
BLACK: 2, 3, 9, 17, KING 10
WHITE: 5, 11, 18, 24, 28 KING 1
TERMS: White to play and win

SOLUTION

18–15, 10-19, 24-15, 9-13———A, 1-6, 2-9, 5-1, 9-14, 1-6, 14-18, 6-9, 18-22———B, 9-14, 17-21, 14-17, 22-25, 17-22, 25-29, 15-10, 21-25, 10-6, 25-30, 6-1, 30-25, 1-6, 25-18, 11-7, 3-10, 6-22———C, White wins.

A———If 9-14, 15-10, 14-18, 10-6, 2-9, 1-6, 9-13, 6-10, etc., White wins.

B———If 18-23, 9-14, 17-21, 14-18, 23-27, 18-22, etc., White wins.

C———Again the "Spread Eagle" idea, which is popular with all grades of players, especially the student. This theme, and the Double Corner Block, seem to hold a fascination for the average player that is insatiable—and the maneuver whereby one holds two *is* instructive as well as entertaining. Although this is a composition, the theme is practical and worthwhile. The composed problem has its place, along with the setting from actual play, but it should not be unnatural.

OPEN-END

(BLACK)

(WHITE)

PROBLEM NUMBER 29
By Henry Toder
BLACK: 5, 6, 9, 12 KING
         31
WHITE: 13, 18, 19, 26
        KING 15
TERMS: White to play and
        win

SOLUTION

26–23, 6-10——A, 15-6, 31-26——B, 6-10, 26-22, 13-6, 22-24, 23-19, 24-15, 10-19——C, White wins.

A——If 31-26, 18-14, 9-27, 19-16, 12-19, 15-22, etc., White wins; if 31-27, 19-16, 12-26, 18-14, 9-18, 15-24, etc., White wins.

B—If 31-27, 6-10, 27-24, 13-6, 24-22, 23-18, White wins. Black is caught in the middle, no matter where he turns.

C——This was Problem No. 102 in Dr. Lewis Schreiber's "Scorpion Club," in *Elam's Checker Board*, April 1966. Out of twenty-seven solutions received, only sixteen were correct. Mr. Toder is Champion of Staten Island, New York, and a great booster of checkers in the metropolitan area. There are scores of players in New York like Henry—virtually unknown nationally—yet able to hold their own with the best of them.

THE SOCKDOLAGER

(BLACK)

(WHITE)

PROBLEM NUMBER 30
By Tom Wiswell
BLACK: 6, 10, 13, 14, 17
WHITE: 7, 25, 29, 30
TERMS: White to play and win

SOLUTION

7-2, 6-9, 2-6, 10-15——A, 6-10, 15-18——B, 25-22—C, 17-26——D, 10-17, 13-22, 30-5, White wins.

A——17-22, 6-15, 13-17, 25-18, 14-23 forms an instructive setting: 29-25, 17-21, 25-22, 9-13, 22-18, 23-27, 18-14, etc., White wins.

B——If 15-19, 25-22, 17-26, 30-16, 14-17, 29-25, 17-21, 25-22, 21-25, 22-18, 25-30, 10-14, or 10-15 and there are three two-for-ones staring Black in the face.

C——The surpise move that brings the game to a dramatic and cleancut conclusion.

D——From a simultaneous exhibition at the YMCA, Knoxville, Tennessee, on January 15, 1964. Many of my problems are fashioned from games played in various displays around the Country.

A VERY NICE ZIRCON

(BLACK)

(WHITE)

PROBLEM NUMBER 31

By Tom Wiswell and John Cary

BLACK: 3, 11, 27, 28 KING 13

WHITE: 12, 30 KINGS 4, 20

TERMS: White to play and draw

SOLUTION

4–8——A, 11-15, 8-11——A, 15-18, 11-15, 18-23, 12-8, 3-12, 20-16, 12-19, 15-31, 13-17, 31-26——B, 23-27, 26-31, 27-32, 30-26, 17-14, 26-23, 14-10, 31-27——C, 10-15, 27-31 ——D, 15-11, 31-27, 11-16, 27-24, 16-20, 24-27——E, etc., drawn.

A——The solution is divided into two parts, of which the first section is "Slocum Forcing" tactics.

B——Now we enter the second phase of the solution: a most unusual "man down" drawing theme.

C——NOT 23-18, 10-7, 18-15, 7-3, 15-11, 32-27, 31-24, 28-32, 24-19, 32-27, 19-15, 27-23, 15-10, 23-18, 11-7, 18-14, 10-17, 3-10, Black wins.

D——If 27-24, 32-27, 24-31, 28-32, 31-27, 15-19, Black wins.

E——This may not be a gem but it could pass for a very nice zircon.

STRATEGIC COMMAND

(BLACK)

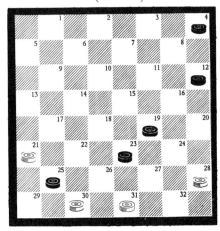

(WHITE)

PROBLEM NUMBER 32

By Tom Wiswell

BLACK: 4, 12, 19, 23, 25
WHITE: 21, 28, 30, 31
TERMS: White to play and draw

SOLUTION

21–17, 25-29, 17-14, 12-16——A, 14-10, 16-20, 10-7, 20-24, 7-3, 23-27, 3-7, 4-8——B, 7-3 (or 7-10), 8-12, 3-7, 27-32——C, 7-10, 32-27, 10-7——D, 12-16, 7-10, 23-27, 10-15, 16-20, 31-26——E, 23-27——F, 15-11, 27-31, 11-16, 31-22, 16-23, 26-22, 28-19, 20-24, 23-18, 26-22, 18-25, 29-22, drawn——G.

A——If 4-8, 14-10, 8-11, 10-7, 11-15, 7-3, 12-16, 3-7, 23-27, 31-24, 16-20, 7-11, etc., drawn.

B——Of course, if 27-32, 7-11, etc., draws easily.

C——If 12-16, 7-10, etc., draws as shown above.

D——NOT 10-15, 19-23, 28-19, 27-24, etc., Black wins.

E——If 15-11, 24-27, 31-15, 20-24, 28-19, 23-7, Black wins.

F——If 29-25, 30-21, 23-30, 21-17, etc., drawn.

G——Not spectacular, perhaps, but instructive, solid Checkers. Pyrotechnics have their place but are no substitute for sound strategy and tactics.

STUDY IN TACTICS

(BLACK)

(WHITE)

PROBLEM NUMBER 33
By Tom Wiswell
BLACK: 4, 5, 7, 10, 28
WHITE: 6, 17, 27, 32
TERMS: White to play and win

SOLUTION

6-2 5-9——A, 2-11, 4-8——B, 11-4, 9-13, 27-23, 13-22, 23-18, 22-26, 4-8, 26-31, 8-12, 31-26, 12-16, 26-31——C, 16-20, 31-26, 20-24, 26-23, 18-15, 10-19, 24-15——D, White wins.

A——Black's best chance, because 7-11, 2-7, 10-15, 7-16, 15-18, 16-19, 5-9 (18-22, 19-23), 17-14, 9-13, 19-15, 18-22, 15-18, 22-26, 27-24, White wins.

B——Of course, if 9-13, 11-7, 13-22, 7-14, etc., White wins.

C——Black is forced to retreat, because 26-23, 18-15, 10-19, 32-27, White wins!

D——The student will note that many games are lost when a man gets stuck in the "dog-hole" (square 28 and square 5), so try your best to keep away from square 28 when you have Blacks and square 5 when you have Whites. To a lesser degree it is also wise to avoid square 12 when you have Whites and square 21 when you have Blacks. These are "dead-end" squares, for obvious reasons.

TRAPPED KING

(BLACK)

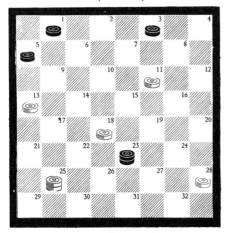

(WHITE)

PROBLEM NUMBER 34
By Leopold and Wiswell
BLACK: 1, 3, 5 KING 23
WHITE: 11, 13, 18, 28
KING 25
TERMS: White to play and
win

SOLUTION

18–14, 23-19——A, 25-21, 19-16——B, 11-7, 3-17, 21-14, 1-6——C, 28-24, 16-11——D, 24-19, 11-7, 19-15 (or 13-9 Now), 7-2, 13-9——E, 6-13, 15-10, White wins.

A——If 23-18, 28-24, 18-9, 13-6, 1-10, 24-19, 5-9, 25-22, etc., White wins.

B——If 19-15, 11-7, 3-17, 21-14, etc., White wins.

C——Otherwise White plays 14-10, etc., and wins.

D——If 16-20, 24-19, 20-24, 19-15, 24-19, 14-10, White wins.

E——Applied science at a critical juncture carries the day: the Black King is imprisoned and the two single men are held to the side of the board.

NEAT, BUT NOT GAUDY

(BLACK)

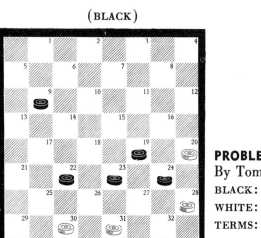

(WHITE)

PROBLEM NUMBER 35
By Tom Wiswell
BLACK: 9, 19, 22, 23, 24
WHITE: 20, 28, 30, 31
TERMS: White to play and
draw

SOLUTION

20–16, 23-27——A, 16-11, 27-32, 11-7, 32-27, 7-2, 27-23, 2-7——B, 23-18, 30-26!——C, 22-25——D, 7-11, 25-29——E, 31-27, 24-31, 11-16, 31-22, 16-5——F, drawn.

A——If 9-13, etc., the White King is back in plenty of time to secure at least a draw.

B——Not 2-6, 9-13, 6-9 (or 6-10), 23-18, etc., Black wins.

C——Black wants 7-11 and a beautiful win by 9-14, 11-16, 19-23! 28-19, 23-27, 31-24, 22-26, 30-23, 18-11, Black wins.

D——Of course, if 9-13, 26-17, 13-22, 7-11, etc., draws.

E——If 9-13, 11-16, 18-23, 26-22, 25-30, 22-18, etc., drawn; if 9-14, 26-22, 18-23, 22-18, 14-17, 11-16, 23-14, 16-23, etc., drawn.

F——I had this position in my manuscript as a White win but took another look at it before giving it to the printer and found the nice escape at note C. The draw may not be so spectacular as the win, but it is more instructive.

THE QUEST

(BLACK)

(WHITE)

PROBLEM NUMBER 36
By Tom Wiswell
BLACK: 5, 11, 28 KING 2
WHITE: 9, 14, 20, 21, 32
TERMS: Black to play, what result?

SOLUTION

11–15, 20-16——A, 15-19, 16-11, 19-23, 11-8, 23-26, 8-3, 26-31, 3-8, 31-26, 8-11, 26-22, 11-15, 22-17——B, 14-10, 5-14, 10-6, 2-9, 15-18, 14-23, 21-5, 23-26, 5-1, 26-31, 1-6, 31-26, 6-10, 26-23, 10-15——C, White wins.

A——21-17 is a wasted move and allows Black to draw the ending. In most problems, economy plays an important part in the winning or drawing strategy and, as in this setting, White is just in time to bring off the desired coup.

B——If 2-7, 9-6, 22-17 (7-2, 14-9), 15-10, 7-2, 14-9 (or 6-1), 5-14, 10-15, 2-9, 15-18, etc., and White wins as in trunk solution.

C——As usual, "Superman" is just in time to foil the villain and score a home-run with the bases loaded. It's a nice thought to know that in checkers we can each be a superman—if we just make the right moves on the board. However, it's comforting to know that even "Superman" cannot win when the other side does not make an error.

TEAM WORK

(BLACK)

(WHITE)

PROBLEM NUMBER 37
By Derek Oldbury and E. A. Harber

BLACK: 25 KINGS 2, 28, 29, 30

WHITE: 10, 31 KINGS 13, 23

TERMS: White to play and win

SOLUTION

13–17——A, 28-24, 17-14, 24-20, 14-18, 20-24, 18-15, 24-28, 15-19, 28-32, 19-24, 32-28, 24-27, 28-32, 31-26, 32-28, 26-22, 28-32, 27-31, 32-28, 22-18, 28-24, 18-15, 24-20, 31-26, 20-16, 26-22, 16-20——B, 15-11, 20-24, 11-8, 24-20, 8-4, 20-24, 4-8, 24-20, 8-11, 20-24, 11-15, 24-28, 15-19, 28-32, 19-24, 32-28, 24-27, 28-32, 22-26, 32-28, 27-32, 28-24, 26-22, 24-28, 22-18, 28-24, 18-15, 24-27, 15-19, 27-18, 19-23, 18-27, 32-23——C, White wins.

A——Not 10-6, which gets White off on the wrong foot.

B——If 16-12, 15-11, 12-16, 22-18, 16-14, 18-9, etc., White wins.

C——Derek Oldbury, the co-author of the fine ending, is, of course, the maverick English master who has held the British, English, and just about every other major title in Great Britain. He was also editor of that iconoclastic magazine, *The Square World,* and authored such works as *Move Over* and, as co-author, *International Draughts and Checkers.* Although losing to Dr. Marion Tinsley and Walter Hellman, he won games from each and held Eugene Frazier even: 2-2-16.

THE PATHFINDER

(BLACK)

(WHITE)

PROBLEM NUMBER 38
By Dr. Lewis F. Schreiber
BLACK: 7, 10, 15 KINGS
          29, 32
WHITE: 13, 28, 30 KING 5
TERMS: White to play and
          draw

SOLUTION

13-9, 10-14——Var. 1, 9-6, 7-11, 6-2, 11-16, 2-7, 14-17
——A, 5-9——B, 16-20——C, 9-14——D, 17-21, 7-11,
15-19, 11-16, 19-23, 16-19, 23-27, 19-24, 27-31, 14-18,
20-27, 18-22, drawn.

A——14-18, 5-9, 16-20, 9-14, 18-23, 7-11, 15-18, 14-17,
23-27, 11-15, 18-23, 17-22, 27-31, 15-19, 23-26, 30-23,
32-27, 22-18, drawn.

B——7-11, 16-20, 11-18, 17-22, 18-25, 29-22, Black wins.

C——32-27, 9-14, 17-22, 30-25, drawn.

D——The trap at note B is still on by 7-11, 32-27, etc.

Var. 1——15-19, 9-6, 7-11, 6-2, 11-16, 2-7, 10-14, 7-11,
16-20, 11-16, 19-23, 16-19——A, 23-27, 19-24——B, 27-31,
5-9, 20-27, 9-18, drawn.

A——If 5-9, 32-27, 9-18, 20-24, 28-19, 27-31, 18-27, 31-15,
Black wins.

B——5-9, 14-18——C, 9-14, 18-22, 30-26, 22-31, 19-24, 29-25, 14-18, 25-21, 18-14, drawn.

C——If 14-17, 19-24, now 27-31 loses by 9-13, but 17-21 draws.

Dr. Schreiber is, of course, the founder of The Scorpion Club, of *Elam's Checker Board* fame, and, with Ben Boland, "Dean of American Problem Editors."

HE ALSO SERVES . . .

(BLACK)

(WHITE)

PROBLEM NUMBER 39
By Tom Wiswell
BLACK: 8, 13, 19, 22, 24
WHITE: 6, 21, 28, 31
TERMS: White to play and draw

SOLUTION

21–17——A, 22-25——B, 17-14, 25-30, 14-10——C, 30-25, 10-7, 13-17——D, 7-3, 8-12, 3-7, 17-22, 7-11, 22-26, 31-22, 25-18, 11-16, 18-23, 6-2——E, 24-27, 16-20, 27-31 (or 23-18), 20-24——F, drawn.

A——White must crown this second man, because 6-2 loses: 6-2, 22-25, 2-7, 25-30, 7-3 (7-10, 30-25), 8-11, 3-7, (3-8, 30-25), 11-15, 7-11 (7-10, 19-23), 15-18, 11-16, 18-23, 16-20——AA, 23-26, 31-22, 30-25, 20-27, 25-18, 27-24, 19-23, 24-20, 23-26, 28-24, 26-31, 20-16, 31-27, 24-20, 27-24, 16-12, Black wins.

AA——If 16-11, 30-25, 11-16, 25-22, 16-11, 22-18, 11-16, 24-27, Black wins.

B——If 22-26, 31-22, 24-27, 17-14, 27-31, 22-18, 31-26, 18-15, 26-22, 6-1, 22-18, 15-11, 8-15, 1-5, 18-9, 5-14, drawn.

C——The man on square 6 must "stand and wait," because with 6-2, 30-25 (threatening 19-23), 14-10, 13-17, 2-7, 17-22, 7-3, 8-12, 3-7, 22-26, etc., Black wins.

D——8-11 and 25-22 are no better; this is Black's best bet.
E——Finally this actor gets his cue: if 16-20, 23-27, 20-16, 19-23, 28-19, 27-24, etc., Black wins.
F——The "delayed steal," a maneuver in timing that must be mastered by the student. Still another ending from actual play.

MIGHTY MONARCH

(BLACK)

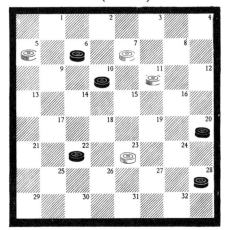

(WHITE)

PROBLEM NUMBER 40
By Dr. Lewis F. Schreiber
BLACK: 6, 10, 20, 22, 28
WHITE: 5, 7, 11, 23
TERMS: White to play and draw

SOLUTION

7–2——A, 6-9, 2-6, 10-15, 6-13, 22-26, 13-17, 26-31, 17-22, 31-27, 23-19!, 15-24, 22-26!——B, C, and the "Mighty Monarch" holds four pieces in a grip.

A——5-1, 22-26, 7-2——A1, 6-9, 1-6, 10-15, 6-13, 26-31, 13-17, 31-26, Black wins.

A1——If 1-5, 10-15, 7-3——A2, 6-10, 5-9, 26-31, Black wins.

A2——If 5-1, 6-10, 1-6, 10-14, Black wins.

B——The continuation requires careful play: 28-32, 5-1, 32-28, 1-6, 27-32, 6-10, 24-27, 10-15, 27-31, 26-23, 28-24, 11-7, 24-27, 15-18, 20-24 (ad lib), 7-2, 24-28, 2-7, 27-24, 7-11, 31-27, 11-15, 24-20, 15-19, 27-24, 18-15, drawn by "Perpetual Check," as they would say in chess.

C——The theme for this composition (colors reversed) was adapted from an end-game problem in the Draughts Column conducted by the former English Champion, Samuel Cohen, in *Reynold's News*, June 13, 1937. The original ending occurred in the second round of the Lincolnshire Championship tournament.

THE UNCOMMON MAN

(BLACK)

(WHITE)

PROBLEM NUMBER 41
By Tom Wiswell
BLACK: 6, 9 KINGS 15, 29
WHITE: 13, 21, 24, 30, 31
TERMS: White to play and
win

SOLUTION

24-19——A, 15-24, 21-17——B, 24-28——C, 31-27——
D, 28-32, 27-24——E, 32-27, 24-19, 27-23, 19-16, 23-19,
16-11, 19-15, 11-7, 15-10, 7-2, 10-15——F, 2-7, 15-19,
7-11, 19-23, 11-15, 23-27, 15-18——G, White wins.

A——This significant sacrifice is the only route to victory.

B——This isolates the King on square 29 and initiates an
attack on the two single men on squares 9 and 6.

C——Because, if 24-19, or 24-20, 31-27, etc., White wins.

D——NOT 31-26, 28-32, 26-22 (26-23, 6-10), 32-27, 22-18,
27-23, 17-14, 6-10!, 14-7, 23-14, 13-6, 14-10, drawn—a
useful life-saver.

E——Note how this uncommon man, in league with "the
move," outwits and outmaneuvers the Black King and forces
the win.

F——Now Napoleon begins "the retreat from Moscow."

G——Proving that mighty monarchs can be vanquished, in
checkers as in politics.

THE BITTER END

(BLACK)

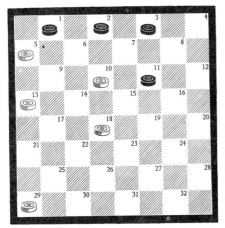

(WHITE)

PROBLEM NUMBER 42
By Tom Wiswell
BLACK: 1, 2, 3, 11
WHITE: 5, 10, 13, 18, 29
TERMS: White to play and win

SOLUTION

13-9——A, 11-16——B, 29-25, 16-20, 25-22, 20-24, 22-17, 24-27, 9-6——C, 2-9, 17-13, 27-31——D, 13-6, 31-26, 6-2, 26-22——E, 2-6, 22-15, 6-2, 15-6, 2-9, 3-7, 9-14, 7-11, 14-18, 11-16, 18-23, 16-20, 23-19, (Or 23-27) 1-6, 5-1, 6-10, 1-6, 10-14, 6-10, 14-18, 10-15, 18-22, 15-18, 22-26, 18-23, 26-30, 19-24, 20-27, 23-32, White wins.

A——White starts the long trek that leads to ultimate victory.

B——If 2-7, 18-14, 11-15, 9-6, etc., White wins.

C——Because 17-13, 2-7, 18-14, 7-11, etc., draws.

D——9-14, 18-9, 27-31, 9-6, 31-26, 6-2, 26-23, 2-7, 23-18, 13-9, 18-15, 9-6, 15-18, 7-11, 18-14, 11-8, 3-12, 6-2, 14-7, 2-11, etc., White wins.

E——26-23, 2-7, 23-14, 7-2, White wins. If 26-31, 10-6, 1-10, 2-6, White wins.

EXPLOITATION

(BLACK)

(WHITE)

PROBLEM NUMBER 43
By Tom Wiswell
BLACK: 7, 19, 23, 24, 28
WHITE: 29, 32 KINGS 14, 30
TERMS: White to play and win

SOLUTION

14-18——A, 24-27, 18-15——B, 27-31——C, 15-24, 23-27——D, 32-23, 28-32, 24-28——E, 32-27, 23-18, 7-10, 29-25, 27-23, 18-14!, 10-17, 25-22!, 17-26, 28-24——F, White wins.

A——When you have an advantage in position you must utilize it to the utmost; that is what White now proceeds to do in a very scientific manner. Watch closely!

B——30-26, 23-30, 32-16, 30-26, etc., only draws.

C——Best, because 19-24, 15-18 and White's "death grip" wins; try it.

D——Black puts up a good fight, but is is not quite enough.

E——Or 23-18 first.

F——White has applied all the pressure possible and comes through with a fine win. The psychological effect of a win like this, on loser and victor alike, is often shattering.

PICKERING PERFECTION

(BLACK)

(WHITE)

PROBLEM NUMBER 44
By S. J. Pickering
BLACK: 5, 12 KINGS 14, 29, 23
WHITE: 9, 20, 31 KINGS 15, 22
TERMS: White to play and draw

SOLUTION

20–16——A, 12-19, 15-24, 23-26——B, 22-17!, 14-21, 31-22, 5-14, 2419!, 29-25——C, 22-17, 14-18, 19-15, 21-14, 15-29——D, etc., drawn.

A——Star move to draw and the beginning of a little beauty that should please expert and student alike.

B——If 14-10, 24-28, 5-14, 22-18, drawn.

C——Of course, if 21-25, 22-18, 14-23, 19-26, etc., drawn by "Perpetual Check."

D——S. J. Pickering was one of England's most prolific problemists, and the quantity was exceeded only by the quality of his brain children. A checker player must have imagination, and a problemist even more so. His flair for brilliant endings and instructive ideas marks him as one of the greats of the problem world and a candidate for the Problemist's Hall of Fame—should one ever be created. The above gem has been published before, but I repeat it here in memory of this genius of the checkerboard.

SHADOW AND SUBSTANCE

(BLACK)

(WHITE)

PROBLEM NUMBER 45
By Tom Wiswell
BLACK: 11, 15, 19 KINGS
           2, 23
WHITE: 28 KINGS 6, 12,
           17, 24
TERMS: White to play and
           win

SOLUTION

17–13——A, 2-9, 13-6, 11-16 (only move) 6-10——
B, 16-20, 24-27!, 23-32, 12-16, 19-24, 10-19, 24-27, 19-24,
27-31, 16-19, 20-27, 19-24——C, White wins.

A——The more natural-looking move (6-10) only draws:
6-10, 11-16 (the life-saver, as 24-20 loses for White), 10-7
(a good try), 2-11, 24-20, 23-27 (NOT 23-18, 17-13, White
wins!), and Black can draw. There are other possibilities for
White, but Black can draw in any case.

B——Of course, if 24-20, 15-18, etc., draws.

C——The key move is, of course, 17-13 at the beginning;
White must resist the temptation to grip Black by 6-10 at
the start. Always look for the "unlikely" move, in problems
AND in games—for they will often lead to a pretty win or
unusual draw. Sometimes the worst-looking move is the best
and the best-looking move is the worst.

THE KNACK

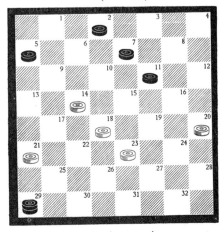

(BLACK)

(WHITE)

PROBLEM NUMBER 46
By Tom Wiswell
BLACK: 2, 5, 7, 11 KING 29
WHITE: 14, 18, 20, 21, 23
TERMS: White to play and draw

SOLUTION

14-9——A, 5-14, 18-9, 11-15, 21-17, 29-25, 17-13, 7-11 ——B, 9-6, 2-9, 13-6, 25-21, 6-1——C, 21-17, 1-5, 17-14, 5-1, 15-18, 23-19, 14-10, 1-6, 10-1, 19-15——D, drawn.

A——If 23-19, 29-25, 19-15, 11-16, 20-11, 7-16, 15-11, 25-22, 18-15, 22-18, 14-10, 16-20, 10-7, 18-23, 7-3, Black wins.

B——If 25-21, 9-6, etc., drawn, as shown in trunk play.

C——If 6-2, 21-17, 2-7, 11-16, 20-11, 15-18, Black wins.

D——The knack of seeing these far-off drawing devices is a skill the student must develop early in his career if he expects to make any real headway with the experts and masters. The ability to look far ahead can be developed in most players, but only with much patience and stick-to-it determination. But once you have conquered the obstacles you will really enjoy playing—and winning—against opponents of real strength.

BLOCK PARTY

(BLACK)

(WHITE)

PROBLEM NUMBER 47
By Tom Wiswell
BLACK: 7, 18, 20, 21 KING 23
WHITE: 8, 25, 28, 30 KING 32
TERMS: White to play and win

SOLUTION

8-3, 7-10——A, 3-7, 10-14——B, 7-10, 14-17, 10-14——C, 17-22, 14-17——D, 22-29, 17-22——D, 18-25, 30-26, 23-30, 28-24, 20-27, 32-23——E, White wins.

A——Black has many doors open to him, but there is "no exit."

If 7-11, 3-7, 11-16 (11-15, 7-10), 7-11, 23-19, 11-15, 19-10, 28-24, White wins.

B——If 18-22, 25-18, 23-14, 7-11, 14-17, 32-27, 17-22, 28-24, 22-17, 24-19, 17-22, 11-15, 10-14, 19-16, etc., White, with "the move," soon wins.

C——If 30-26, 21-30 (NOT 23-30), 26-19, 18-22, 10-14, 17-21, 28-24, 20-27, 32-23, 22-25, 14-17, 25-29, 17-22, 30-25, 23-18, etc., only draws. Black has "the move" and in this case that is good, for White can win now.

D——Black cannot escape his fate and the game comes to a sensational and instructive conclusion.

E——Based on an actual game at The New York Club, although a change was necessary in order to omit a dual solution.

SHOCK TREATMENT

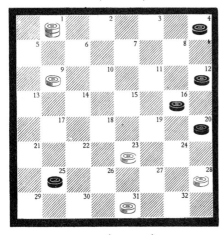

(WHITE)

PROBLEM NUMBER 48
By Tom Wiswell
BLACK: 4, 12, 16, 20, 25
WHITE: 9, 23, 28, 31 KING
1
TERMS: White to play and win

SOLUTION

1-6, 4-8——A, 6-10, 8-11——B, 10-14, 11-15, 14-17, 25-30, 31-27——C, 30-26——D, 9-5, 26-19, 17-22——E, White wins.

A——If 16-19, 23-16, 12-19, 31-27, 4-8, 6-10, 8-11, 10-7, 11-15, 7-11, 19-23, 11-18, 23-32, 18-23, White wins.

B——With this, Black is threatening 20-24, etc.

C——This type of move usually "shocks" your opponent, for it seldom figures in his calculations and he is unprepared to meet it.

D——Of course, if 30-25, 23-18, and if 15-19, 17-22, White wins.

E——The deciding game in a six-game heat with my frequent opponent, George Moore, New York expert and National tourney player of note (April 21, 1964).

DOUBLE TROUBLE

(BLACK)

(WHITE)

PROBLEM NUMBER 49
By John Smarra
BLACK: 2 3, 8, 18 KING 29
WHITE: 10, 12, 15, 26
            KING 1
TERMS: White to play and
            draw

SOLUTION

10-6——A, 2-9, 1-6, 29-25——B, 6-13, 25-21——C, 26-
22, 18-25, 13-9, 21-17, 15-10! (threatening 9-6), 8-11, 10-
7——E, 3-10, 9-14, drawn.

A——Of course, if 1-5, 2-7, 10-6, 7-10, etc., Black wins.

B——Because 9-13, 15-10, etc. allows an easy draw.

C——If 25-30, 26-22——D, 18-25, 13-9, 30-26, 9-6, etc.,
drawn.

D——NOT 26-23, 18-27, 13-9, 30-26, 9-6, 26-23, 15-10, 27-
32, 10-7, 3-10, 6-15, 32-28, 12-3, 23-19, 15-24, 28-19, Black
wins.

E——By the versatile New York composer who, with Dr.
Lewis Schreiber, conducted the Scorpion Club of *Elam's
Checkerboard* fame. Most of the world's best problemists
have submitted positions to this noted department. Ben Boland, Chris Nelson, A. J. Mantell, Matt Long, Bill Scott,
Arthur Gladstone, Milton Johnson, Louis Cowie, James
Keene, George Brown, Jerry Childers, Calhoun Clinkscales,
and the writer are just a few of the composers who have
participated in the Scorpion Club.

KNOCKOUT DROPS

(BLACK)

(WHITE)

PROBLEM NUMBER 50
By Tom Wiswell
BLACK: 1, 20, 25 KINGS 2, 19
WHITE: 13, 15, 17, 21, 28 KING 30
TERMS: White to play and win

SOLUTION

13-9——A, 19-10, 17-14——B, 10-17, 21-14, 25-29——C, 14-10——D, 1-5——E, 30-26——F, 5-14, 26-22——F, 29-25, 22-29, 14-18, 29-25, 18-23, 25-22, 23-27, 22-18, 27-31, 18-23——G, White wins.

A——If 15-11, 19-23, 11-8, 25-29, etc., leaves Black well situated.

B——White doesn't appear too strong, but wait and see what happens.

C——Of course, if 1-6, 30-21, 6-13, 14-10, White wins.

D——Black has two Kings but this move nullifies the power of the monarchs and forces matters nicely.

E——29-25, 30-21, 1-5, 21-25, 5-14, 25-22, White wins.

F——Note this theme, for it will allow you to win many games a piece short—to the consternation of your opponent.

G——Based on a game from a New York Knockout Tournament played in 1968, but the theme is basic.

THREAT AND EXECUTION

(BLACK)

(WHITE)

PROBLEM NUMBER 51
By Tom Wiswell

BLACK: 3, 8, 9, 20 KING 16
WHITE: 5, 12, 18, 28, 31
TERMS: White to play and draw

SOLUTION

28–24 (necessary), 20-27, 31-24, 16-20 (best), 24-19, 20-16, 19-15, 16-19, 15-10, 19-23——A, 10-7——B, 23-14, 5-1——B, 3-10, 12-3——C, 9-13——D, 1-6——E, 10-15, 6-10——E, 14-7, 3-19, etc., drawn——F

A——If 8-11, 5-1, 19-23, 10-7 (or 18-15), drawn.

B——The beginning of the "threat" that secures White's draw.

C——Now we come to the "execution" of the "threat."

D——Or 10-15; it makes no difference.

E——Executing the threat, from which there is no escape.

F——The master and the expert utilize the "threat and execution" policy many times—but remember, the threat is sometimes worse than the execution! Learn to distinguish between the genuine threat and the one that is "pure bluff." At the same time, never shrink from using the latter yourself; you'll be surprised how often it works.

BEEBE'S BLACK BEAUTY

(BLACK)

(WHITE)

PROBLEM NUMBER 52
By Clayton Beebe
BLACK: 2, 10, 12, 16 KING 31
WHITE: 17, 18, 24, 28 KING 1
TERMS: Black to play and win

SOLUTION

31-27——A, 1-6——B, 2-9, 17-13, 27-20, 13-6, 16-19——C, 6-2, 20-16——C, 2-7, 19-24!——D, 7-14, 16-19——E, Black wins.

A——The beginning of a beautiful conception, by the Illinois Checker Champion, from Peoria.

B——White hopes to draw with this, but it is an "optical illusion."

C——Black now puts his brilliant plan into execution—and thereby executes White.

D——If you saw this move at "A," then you have made real progress as a problem-solver—providing you did not "peek."

E——The author has been Illinois State Champion several times and in 1969 scored his greatest victory, winning the American Checker Federation's 6th District tourney—where he defeated such greats as Everett Fuller, Boby Martin, and La Verne Dibble in successive heats! Mr. Beebe is not only a champion *at* checkers, he is also a champion *of* checkers, being General District Manager for the ACF.

DOUBLE-"CORNERED"

(BLACK)

(WHITE)

PROBLEM NUMBER 53
By Tom Wiswell

BLACK: 5, 18, 20, 23 KING
10

WHITE: 8, 9, 16, 27 KING
32

TERMS: White to play and
draw

SOLUTION

9–6, 10-1, 7-3, 1-6, 3-7, 5-9, 16-12, 9-14, 7-11, 6-10, 11-16, 10-15, 16-11——A, 15-8, 12-3——B, 14-17, 3-7, 17-22, 7-10, 22-26, 10-14!——C, 26-31——D, 32-28, 23-32, 14-23, 31-27, 23-19, 27-31, 19-23——E, drawn.

A——White is forced to exchange and the resulting position does not look too good—but all is not yet lost, as you will see.

B——White is already one man down and the piece on square 27 is vulnerable—but White is not discouraged because he has a plan. That is always the important thing: Have a plan!

C——Not 10-15, 26-31, etc., Black wins.

D——If 26-30, 14-17, 30-26, 17-14, etc., also draws.

E——Black is double-"cornered"! This was White's plan from the diagram and it neatly saves the situation.

UNCOMMON SENSE

(BLACK)

(WHITE)

PROBLEM NUMBER 54
By Tom Wiswell
BLACK: 9, 15, 19 KINGS
29, 32
WHITE: 21, 26, 28, 30
KING 22
TERMS: White to play and win

SOLUTION

21-17——A, 9-13——B, 17-14, 32-27, 14-9——C, 27-31, 26-23——D, 19-26, 30-23, 31-27, 23-19, 15-24, 28-19, 27-23——E, 19-16, 23-19——E, 16-11, 19-15——E, 11-7, 15-10——E, 9-5——F, 10-3, 5-1, 3-7, 1-6——G, White wins.

A——If 22-17, either 9-13 or 32-27 will suffice for Black.

B——32-27, 17-13, 9-14, 13-9, 27-32 (if 14-18, 26-23 and if 27-31, 22-25), 26-23, 19-26, 22-31, etc., White wins.

C——If 14-10, 27-23, 10-6, 23-18, 6-2, 18-25, 30-21, etc., drawn.

D——If 9-6, 13-17, etc., draws.

E——Black's only hope now is to reach square 17—and a draw.

F——But by exercising uncommon checker sense White frustrates Black with this basic "spread eagle" theme.

G——Good to the last drop!

EXTRA DUTY

(BLACK)

(WHITE)

PROBLEM NUMBER 55
By Tom Wiswell and Jimmy
Ricca
BLACK: 3, 5, 6, 12 KING 4
WHITE: 11, 16, 19, 20, 25
TERMS: White to play and
draw

SOLUTION

25–22, 5-9——A, 11-8——B, 4-11, 16-7, 3-10, 20-16——C,
10-14, 16-11, 9-13, 11-7, 6-9, 7-2, 14-17, 22-18, 17-22 (or
17-21), 2-6, 22-26——D, 6-10, 26-31, (or 26-30) 10-15!!
——E, drawn.

A——If 6-9, 22-17, etc.

B——If 22-18, 9-13, 18-14, 3-8, 11-7, 6-10, 14-9, 8-11, 7-2,
11-15, Black wins.

C——It appears that White will be too late to do anything—
but wait!

D——The Black man can crown on 29, 30, or 31 and the
result is still a draw by the theme shown.

E——NOT 10-14, 31-26, 14-5, 26-23, etc., Black wins. Com-
pare this problem with No. 23 (by Wiswell) in *Checker
Magic*. Jimmy Ricca is the well-known New York master who
has won many important tournaments around the country.
He has an avid interest in end-game play.

TOP-DRAWER

(BLACK)

(WHITE)

PROBLEM NUMBER 56
By Tom Wiswell
BLACK: 1, 3, 7, 20, 21
WHITE: 14, 15, 18, 26, 29
TERMS: White to play and draw

SOLUTION

14–9——A, 20-24, 26-23, 24-27, 23-19, 1-5——B, 9-6, 27-31, 6-2, 7-11, 15-8, 3-12, 2-6——C, 31-26, 6-10!, 26-23, 18-14, 23-16, 10-15, 16-20, 15-19, drawn.

A——15-10 loses easily, as an examination will show.

B——27-31 forms another instructive position: 27-31, 9-6, 1-10, 15-6, 31-26 (31-27, 19-16), 18-15, 26-22, 6-2, 22-18, 2-11, 3-8, 11-4, 18-11, 4-8, 11-4, 19-15, 4-8, 15-10, 8-11, 10-6, 11-15, 6-1, 15-18, 1-6, 18-22, 6-10, 21-25, 10-15, drawn. The student should note this idea.

C——The men on squares 18 and 19 must "stay put," for any attempt to move them would result in disaster for White.

A GRIPPING PROBLEM

(BLACK)

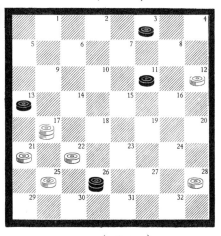

(WHITE)

PROBLEM NUMBER 57
By Tom Wiswell
BLACK: 3, 11, 13 KING 26
WHITE: 12, 21, 22, 25, 28
KING 17
TERMS: White to play and win

SOLUTION

28–24——A, 11-15, 24-20, 15-19——B, 20-16, 19-24, 16-11, 24-27, 11-8, 27-31, 8-4, 31-27, 4-8, 27-23, 8-11, 23-19 ——C, 17-14!——D, 26-10, 11-15——E, White wins.

A——Although White is two men ahead, the actual win is not apparent until the final flourish at note D; Black's grip on the White men in the single corner is very real and presents a nice problem.

B——15-18 leaves White still a man ahead and "the move" to win: 15-18, 22-15, 13-29, 21-17, 26-22, 17-13, 22-18, 15-10, 18-15, 10-6, 15-11, 6-2, 29-25, 13-9, 25-22, 9-6, 22-18, 6-1, 18-15, 1-6, 15-19, 6-10, 19-23, 10-14, 23-19, 14-18, 19-15, 18-23, 15-10, 23-19, 10-14, 2-6, etc., White wins.

C——Black must move to the very square that defeats him; if 23-27, 11-15, 27-24, 15-10, 24-19, 17-14, 26-17, 14-9 (or 14-18), White wins.

D——At last White breaks free from the iron grip!

E——From a mail game played with Parks Herzog, the Colorado expert, during 1967. We drew the actual game, but this was a possible variation.

85

POCKET OF GOLD

(BLACK)

(WHITE)

PROBLEM NUMBER 58
By Tom Wiswell
BLACK: 1, 2, 3, 21 KING 30
WHITE: 14, 20, 22, 27, 29, 31
TERMS: White to play and win

SOLUTION

22–17——A, 21-25——B, 29-22, 30-25, 14-9, 25-18, 27-23, 18-27, 31-24, 1-5, 17-14, 3-7, 24-19——C, 7-11, 19-16, 11-15, 16-11, 15-19, 11-8, 19-23, 8-3, 23-26, 3-8, 26-30, 20-16——D, 30-26, 16-11, 26-22, 11-7, 2-11, 8-15, 22-17, 15-10, 17-13, 10-6, 13-17, 14-10, 5-14, 6-9, 14-18, 9-14 ——E, White wins.

A——NOT 22-18, 21-25, 29-22, 30-26, etc., and White cannot win.

B——Black's best chance to draw, and he almost does just that; moving any of the King-row men is a waste of time, since White wins easily.

C——White's only move, but it is more than sufficient.

D——Moving the King 8-11, etc., only draws; White must trade off the man on square 2 and thus escape the bind on the pieces on squares 9 and 14.

E——The old reliable "pocket" theme, so called for obvious reasons. When you *know* the theme, everything is easy: "Every door is barred with gold, and opens but to golden keys" (Tennyson).

THE THREE WAITERS

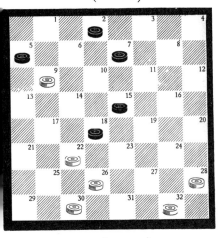

(BLACK)

(WHITE)

PROBLEM NUMBER 59
By Tom Wiswell
BLACK: 2, 5, 7, 15, 18
WHITE: 9, 22, 26, 28, 30,
        32
TERMS: White to play and
        win

SOLUTION

30–25——A, 5-14, 28-24——B, 2-6, 32-28 (or 24-20), 6-9,
24-20, 9-13, 20-16, 14-17, 28-24 (16-12, 7-11), 17-21——C,
16-12, 21-30 (No. 1), 12-8, 18-25 (No. 2), 8-3, 30-23 (No.
3), 3-26, 13-17, 26-30, 25-29, 24-20, 17-21, 20-16, 29-25,
30-26——D, etc., White wins.

A——The start of a pretty combination play by White.

B——NOT 32-27, because Black replies with 7-11!

C——If 15-19, 22-15——CC, 19-28, 25-21, 17-22, 26-17,
13-22, 21-17, 28-32, 17-14, 32-27, 15-11, White wins.

CC——NOT 24-15, 17-21, 15-11, 21-30, 22-15, 30-23, 11-2,
23-19, drawn.

D——This is a good example of forced checkers from note
A to the exciting wind-up. White now holds the Black King
and single man at bay and returns with his second King to
complete the win.

I suggest that, after solving each problem, you reset the position and go over the solution again and again—for a gain!

FORCING THE ISSUE

(BLACK)

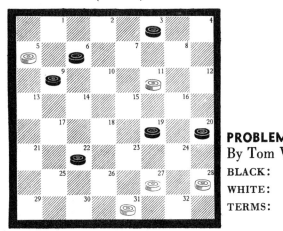

(WHITE)

PROBLEM NUMBER 60
By Tom Wiswell
BLACK: 3, 6, 9, 19, 20, 22
WHITE: 5, 11, 27, 28, 31
TERMS: White to play and win

SOLUTION

27-24——A, 20-27, 31-15, 9-13——B, 5-1——C, 6-9, 1-5, 9-14, 5-9, 14-17, 9-14, 17-21, 14-17, 22-25——D, 17-22, 25-29, 15-10, 21-25, 10-6, 25-30, 6-1, 30-25, 1-6, 25-18, 11-7, 3-10, 6-22——E, White wins.

A——This brings the issue to a head and does not allow Black any escape; if 5-1, 19-23!, 27-18, 6-10, etc., Black draws.

B——Or 9-14, with the same result.

C——Now we get a good example of "forced checkers," in the real sense of the word.

D——If 22-26, 17-22, 26-31, 15-10, 31-27, 10-6, 27-23, 28-24, 27-23, 24-19, 27-24, 19-16 (quickest), 24-19, 6-1, 19-12, 1-6, White wins.

E——Based on an actual game played at The Chess and Checker Club of New York on February 8, 1967.

LONG LIVE THE KING

(BLACK)

(WHITE)

PROBLEM NUMBER 61
By George L. King
BLACK: 1, 2, 4, 10 KING
24
WHITE: 9, 11, 13, 21, 22,
31
TERMS: White to play and
win

SOLUTION

9–6, 2-9, 13-6, 10-14——A, 6-2, 24-19——B, 31-27, 14-18——C, 22-15, 19-10——D, 27-24, 1-5, 24-19, 5-9——E, 21-17, 9-13, 19-15——F, 10-19, 2-7, 13-22, 11-8, 4-11, 7-23——G, White wins.

A——Black, although a man down, has visions of drawing, but White will not be denied in this instructive end-game of perfect timing.

B——Stopping 2-7 and 22-17 and restricting White's movements.

C——Preparing to threaten the man on square 11.

D——A very fine position requiring timing and imagination.

E——If 10-7, 19-15, 7-16, 15-11, etc., White wins by "first position."

F——Allowing the White King to come to the rescue!

G——George L. King of Detroit was a valued member of The Scorpion Club and contributed many fine positions to *Elam's Checker Board* before his death on May 12, 1967.

DON'T TOUCH THE PIECES

(BLACK)

(WHITE)

PROBLEM NUMBER 62

By Tom Wiswell

BLACK: 12, 13, 16, 20
KING 6

WHITE: 15, 19, 23, 25, 27, 29

TERMS: White to play and win

SOLUTION

25–22, 6-9, 29-25, 9-14, 22-18, 14-17——A, 18-14, 17-10, 15-6, 13-17, 6-2, 17-21, 25-22, 21-25, 2-7, 25-30——B, 7-11, 30-26——C, 11-15——D, 26-17, 15-18, 17-13, 18-14——E, White wins.

A——If 14-9, 25-22, 9-6, etc., White runs Black out of moves.

B——Black has his eye on all those White single pieces and it looks like he will surely draw—but appearances are deceiving.

C——If 30-25, 19-15, 25-18, 23-14, etc., White wins.

D——The play that robs Black of his "draw."

E——Not a masterpiece, perhaps, but an idea well worthy of note. One must master many simple ideas to understand the difficult end-game in checkers.

THE "WASTED" MOVE

(BLACK)

(WHITE)

PROBLEM NUMBER 63
Tom Wiswell *vs.* John Cary
BLACK: 6, 10, 14, 16, 20, 24
WHITE: 11, 17, 21, 23, 31
TERMS: White to play and draw

SOLUTION

11–7, 24-27——A, 31-24, 20-27, 7-2, 6-9, 2-6——B, 27-31, 6-13——C, 31-27, 23-19, 16-23, 13-9, 14-18, 9-14, 10-15, 17-13!——D, 27-24 (15-19, 14-10), 14-10, 24-19, 10-14, 19-16, 14-10——E, etc., drawn.

A——If 6-9, 7-2, 9-13, 2-6, 13-22, 6-15, 24-27, 31-24, 20-27, 15-19!, drawn.

B——If 17-13, 10-15, 13-6, 15-19, etc., Black wins.

C——Of course, if 6-15, 31-27, Black wins.

D——White is forced to "waste" a move, for if 14-10, 27-31, Black wins. As a rule, in "man-down" positions like this it is fatal to lose even one. move, but in this case White still manages to scrape through.

E——From a practice game with my frequent sparring partner, Brooklyn expert John Cary. I thought I had him in this game, but it never pays to count your checkers until they're hatched.

THE KANSAS CYCLONE

(BLACK)

(WHITE)

PROBLEM NUMBER 64
By Tom Wiswell

BLACK: KINGS 13, 22, 26, 27, 28

WHITE: 8, 10, 17 KINGS 5, 19, 20

TERMS: White to play and win

SOLUTION

10–7——A, 22-25——B, 17-14, 13-9——B, 19-24!——C, 28-19, 20-16!——C, 19-17——D, 5-32——E, White wins.

A——This is White's only move to win; for example: 19-15, 22-25, 17-14, 13-9, etc., draws.

B——Since Black is a man down, he has nothing better than to try and regain his piece; therefore, these moves are logical for him.

C——One New York player described these moves as "high camp"!

D——Or, Black has the choice of losing by 9-18, 16-21, etc.

E——No, I wasn't on a "trip" via LSD when I composed this problem, regardless of what you may think. I got the basic idea from an ending between two players at the New York Chess and Checker Club (where anything can happen—and usually does) and just searched until I found a suitable setting with which I could frame the idea. This is a favorite of the noted Jules Leopold.

DOWN MEMORY LANE

(BLACK)

(WHITE)

PROBLEM NUMBER 65
By Tom Wiswell

BLACK: 13, 16, 20 KINGS 7, 22

WHITE: 15, 18, 23, 27, 28 KING 1

TERMS: White to play and win

SOLUTION

15–10——A, 7-14——B, 18-9, 22-26——C, 1-6, 26-19, 6-10, 13-17, 9-6, 17-22, 6-2, 22-26, 2-7, 26-31——D, 7-11, 31-24, 11-15!——E, White wins.

A——Necessary; if 18-14, for example, 7-3, etc., only draws.

B——The novice will note that 22-6, 1-3, etc., White wins.

C——To delay by 13-17 does not help Black in any way.

D——If 26-30, 7-11, 30-26, 11-15, White wins.

E——Reminiscent of the win Professor W. R. Fraser missed on me in our 1956 title match at free-style checkers at Glasgow, Kentucky: Black 11, 12, 15 Kings 21, 27 White 20, 24 Kings 2, 10 Black to play and win: 21-25, 10-19, 25-30, 2-7, 30-26, 7-16, 27-23! Black wins. We were playing by clock and, with only seconds to go, Bill offered me a draw and Dr. Marion Tinsley later pointed out the win. Since I won the forty-game match by two to nothing, this was a significant "draw" for me.

MAJORITY RULE

(BLACK)

(WHITE)

PROBLEM NUMBER 66
By Tom Wiswell

BLACK: 2, 9, 14 KINGS 3, 16

WHITE: 11, 15, 21, 22, 29 KING 1

TERMS: White to play and win

SOLUTION

1–6——A, 16-7, 6-13, 2-6——B, 13-17——C, 14-18——D, 17-13——E, 18-25, 29-22, 3-8 (if 7-2, 15-11), 22-18, 8-3, 21-17, 7-10, 15-11, 10-15, 11-7!, 15-22, 7-2, 6-10——F, 2-6, 10-15, 13-9, 22-13, 6-1, White wins.

A——The only move to win; if 11-8, 3-12, 1-5, 16-19, 15-10, 12-8, Black has no trouble in drawing, at least.

B——A good move, threatening the man on square 15. If, instead, Black plays 14-18, then 13-9, etc., is an easy win.

C——If 29-25, or 22-17, 14-18, etc., draws.

D——If 6-9, 17-10, 7-14, 22-17, 14-18, 17-13, etc., White wins.

E——If 29-25, 18-23, etc., draws easily.

F——If 6-9, 13-6, 22-13, 6-9, 13-6, 2-9, White wins on "the move."

THE LAST WORD

PROBLEM NUMBER 67
By Tom Wiswell

BLACK: 12, 28 KINGS 22, 24, 26

WHITE: 6, 8, 10, 23, 30, 32

TERM: White to play and win

SOLUTION

23–18——A, 22-15, 30-23, 15-11——B, 8-4, 24-27, 23-18, 27-23, 6-2!——C, 23-7, 4-8!, 11-4, 2-11——D, 4-8, 11-4, 12-16, 4-8——E, White wins.

A——NOT 23-19, 24-15, 30-23, 15-11 (or 22-26), 8-4, 22-26, 23-18, 26-22, draws.

B——If 24-27, 23-19, 15-24, 32-23, etc., White wins.

C——Giving up three men for one in return, but generosity pays off where positional play is sufficient to carry the day. It isn't how many men you have, but where they are, that counts.

D—Black must give up the King or the single man, but in either case White ends up with "the move" and the last word.

E——From a simultaneous exhibition by the writer at Statesville, North Carolina, March 24, 1968. These displays provide many ideas for problems.

UNHAPPY ENDING

(BLACK)

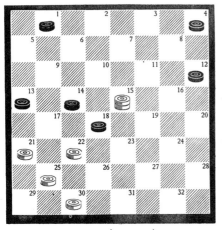

(WHITE)

PROBLEM NUMBER 68
By Tom Wiswell
BLACK: 1, 4, 12, 13, 14, 18
WHITE: 21, 22, 25, 30
KING 15
TERMS: White to play and win

SOLUTION

15–19, 12-16——A, 19-12, 18-23, 22-18——B, 1-5, 18-9, 5-14, 25-22——B, 23-27, 12-16——C, 4-8, 16-12, 8-11, 12-8, 11-15——D, 8-11, 14-18, 21-17!——E, 18-25, 30-21, 13-22, 11-25——F, White wins.

A——Black's best chance; anything else loses quickly—on position.

B——These moves are forceful and bring about the desired result.

C——Threatening to steal the man on square 14.

D——If 14-18, 8-15, 18-25, 15-18, 25-29, 18-22, 27-31, 21-17, 31-27, 17-14, 27-24, 14-9, 24-19, 9-6, 19-15, 6-2, etc., White wins.

E——NOT 30-25, 18-23, 11-18, 27-23, 18-27, 32-23, or White's win has suddenly disappeared.

F——While this is a composition, it is based on an actual ending from another exhibition game. Sometime if you lose or win a game with a neat idea, but feel it is too easy, just try setting it back and you will soon have a worthwhile problem.

QUICKSAND

(BLACK)

(WHITE)

PROBLEM NUMBER 69
By Tom Wiswell
BLACK: 2, 6, 21 KINGS 10, 18
WHITE: 8, 11, 17, 25, 27, 30
TERMS: White to play and win

SOLUTION

8–3———A, 6-9, 3-8———B, 9-13———C, 27-23!———D, 18-27, 17-14———D, 10-17, 25-22, 17-26, 30-23, 27-18, 11-7, 2-11, 8-22———E, White wins.

A———If 27-24, 6-9, 17-13, 10-14, 13-6, 2-9, 8-3, 9-13, 3-7, 14-17, drawn.

B———Again, if 17-13, 10-14, 13-6, 2-9, etc., draws.

C———2-6———CC, 17-13, 9-14, 8-3, 14-17, 11-7, 10-14, 3-8, 14-9, 8-11, 9-5, 7-2, 5-9, 2-7, 9-5, 25-22, 18-25, 7-10, 6-15, 11-18, etc., White wins. (Jules Leopold and Tom Wiswell)

CC———If 10-7, 8-12, 7-16, 12-19, 9-13, 19-23, 13-29, 23-14, 29-25, 14-17, White wins.

D———Based on a game with Billy Grolz, played January 25, 1968. Billy, a brilliant New York expert, saw the win and avoided trouble earlier.

E———The student will note that after Black gives up one man, say 21-25, 22-29, White has "the move" on the remaining man. Remember: It is better to be a "man down" and a "game up" than a "man up" and a "game down."

TURNING THE TABLES

(BLACK)

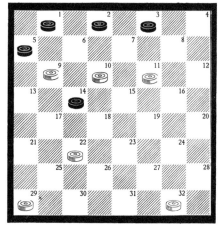

(WHITE)

PROBLEM NUMBER 70
By Tom Wiswell
BLACK: 1, 2, 3, 5, 14
WHITE: 9, 10, 11, 22, 29, 32
TERMS: White to play and win

SOLUTION

9–6!——A, 2-9, 29-25, 9-13, 25-21, 5-9, 10-6!!——B, 1-10, 32-27, 10-15, 27-23——C, White wins.

A——Necessary, if 29-25 (or 32-27), 14-18, 22-15, 5-14, etc., draws.

B——Snatching victory from the jaws of defeat with a judicious and timely sacrifice. White has completely turned the tables!

C——Of course, "the move" also aids in the final victory. Here is a neat position by an unknown author:

> BLACK: 9, 11, KINGS 13, 26
> WHITE: 21, 24 KINGS 4, 32
> TERMS: White to play and win
> SOLUTION

4-8, 11-15, 8-11, 15-18, 11-15, 26-22, 21-17, 18-23, 15-18, 22-15, 32-28, 13-22, 24-19, 15-24, 28-17, White wins.

A HALF-NELSON

(BLACK)

(WHITE)

PROBLEM NUMBER 71
By Tom Wiswell and Chris Nelson

BLACK: 2, 3, 5, 15 KING 32

WHITE: 10, 12, 13, 25, 26, 27

TERMS: White to play and win

SOLUTION

27–24——A, 32-27, 24-20, 27-31, 26-22——B, 31-26 (nothing better), 25-21——C, 26-17, 21-14, 15-19, 20-16——D, 19-23, 16-11, 23-26, 11-8, 26-30, 8-4, 30-26, 4-8, 26-22, 8-11, 22-17——E, 10-7——F, 17-10, 11-8, 2-11, 8-6——G, White wins.

A——If 26-23, 15-18, 23-14, 32-23, draws, as shown elsewhere (Strategic Command position).

B——25-22, 5-9, 13-6, 2-9, 22-18, 31-22, 18-11, 22-18, 10-6, 18-15, etc., drawn.

C——If 22-17, 15-18, 25-21, 26-22, 20-16, 18-23, 16-11, 5-9, 13-6, 22-13, 6-1, 13-9, 1-5, 9-14, etc., drawn.

D——13-9, 19-23, 10-6, 23-26, 6-1, 26-30, 1-6, 30-26, 6-10, 26-22, drawn.

E——If 22-18, 13-9, 18-22, 11-15, 22-17, 9-6, 2-18, 15-13, White wins.

F——The two-for-two might be termed an "optical illusion." White could delay this, but "eventually, why not now?"

G——Chris Nelson is a real "old timer" who, along with Newell Banks, Harry Lieberman, and one or two others, represents "yesteryear."

THE PLOT

(BLACK)

(WHITE)

PROBLEM NUMBER 72
By Tom Wiswell
BLACK: 1, 3, 6, 8 KING 29
WHITE: 10, 12, 16, 17, 19
21
TERMS: White to play and
win

SOLUTION

19–15——A, 29-25——B, 17-14——C, 25-22——D, 21-17
——E, 22-13, 14-9, 13-17, 9-2, 17-14, 2-7, 14-18——F,
15-11——G, 8-15, 12-8——G, 3-19, 10-6, 1-10, 7-16, 15-18,
16-19, White wins.

A——Of course, the beginner will not that 10-7, 3-10, 12-3,
10-14, draws.

B——Since Black is a piece short, all his moves in the story
are dictated and he cannot play out of character. Every
problem has a plot, much like an Agatha Christie mystery,
and the solver must try to unravel the riddle.

C——If 16-11, 25-22, 11-4, 22-13, etc., drawn.

D——Ironically, the only plausible move; if 25-30, 16-11,
White wins.

E——The key to the mystery and the plot begins to unfold.

F——This surely draws—but does it?

G——The culminating moves, which you should have seen
at note A—if you are an expert solver.

TIME AND SPACE

(BLACK)

(WHITE)

PROBLEM NUMBER 73
By Tom Wiswell

BLACK: 7, 12, 16, 20 KING 21

WHITE: 14, 23, 24, 27, 29, 31

TERMS: White to play and win

SOLUTION

23–18——A, 21-17——B, 29-25——C, 17-10, 18-14——
C, 10-17, 25-22——C, 17-26, 31-22——D, 16-19——E, 24-
15, 12-16, 22-18, 16-19, 18-14, 19-24, 27-23, 24-27, 23-19,
27-31, 19-16, 31-26, 15-11——F, White wins.

A——Of course, if 14-9, 21-17, 9-6, 7-10, 6-2, 10-15, etc.,
draws.

B——If 7-11, 14-10, 21-17, 31-26, etc., White wins.

C——White gives up three checkers for one, but in doing so
obtains a winning ending. Learn to utilize your position and
material to the fullest, especially in the end-game.

D——Although one down, White must get two men back
for his investment.

E——Of course, if 7-10 or 7-11, 22-18, wins at once for
White.

F——Another ending from actual play. Don't listen to those
cynics who will tell you these endings never arise in crossboard play; I have seen it happen again and again, as it
will in the future.

THE TIME MACHINE

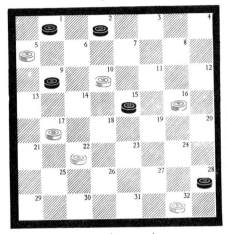

(BLACK)

(WHITE)

PROBLEM NUMBER 74
By Tom Wiswell
BLACK: 1, 2, 9, 15, 28
WHITE: 5, 10, 16, 17, 22
32
TERMS: White to play and
win

SOLUTION

17–13, 9-14, 13-9, 15-19, 16-11——A, 19-23, 22-18——
B, 23-26, 18-15, 26-31, 11-8, 31-26, 15-11, 26-22, 8-3,
22-17——C, 3-8, 17-13——D, 10-6, 1-10, 5-1, 13-6, 11-7,
2-11, 8-15, 10-19, 1-17——E, White wins.

A——If 10-6, 1-10, 5-1, 10-15, 1-6, 14-18, 22-17, 18-22,
6-10, 22-26 (threatening 19-23, etc.), 17-13, 26-31, 9-6, 2-9,
13-6, 31-26, 6-2, 26-22, 2-7 (if 16-12, 15-18), 15-18, 7-11,
18-23, etc., drawn.

B——If 11-8, 23-26, etc., drawn.

C——If 22-18, 3-8, 18-15, 10-6, 1-10, 5-1, 14-17, 8-4, 15-8,
4-11, 10-14, 1-6, 17-21, 6-10, 14-17, 10-14, 17-22, 14-17,
22-25, 17-22, 25-29, 22-26, White wins.

D——Black gets his man back but is caught in an instructive
"mating net" in the process.

E——I call this "The Time Machine" for obvious reasons,
and the student should study the precision and exactitude
employed by White in attaining his goal.

THE DRAWING BOARD

PROBLEM NUMBER 75
By Tim Wiswell
BLACK: 1, 5, 18, 21, 22
           KING 32
WHITE: 8, 16, 20, 27, 29,
           31
TERMS: White to play and
           draw

SOLUTION

27–24, 32-28, 24-19, 28-24, 16-11, 24-15, 8-4, 15-8, 4-11,
18-23, 11-15, 23-26, 15-19, 26-30, 19-23, 5-9, 20-16——A,
9-14, 16-11, 1-6, 11-7, 6-9, 7-2, 9-13, 2-6, 14-17, 6-10——
B, 22-26, 31-22, 17-26, 10-15, 26-31, 15-19, 31-26, 29-25
——C, 26-31, 19-24, etc., drawn——D.

A——NOT 23-18, 30-26, 18-25, 21-30, 31-22, 9-14, Black
wins.

B——NOT 23-27, 22-25, 29-22, 17-26, 31-22, 30-26, Black
wins.

C——The key to the White draw and effective check of
Black's attempt at "majority rule"!

D——Losing losses is rather easy, but winning wins and
drawing draws often require considerable ingenuity. The
right themes are all there, just waiting to be discovered.
With some study and patience you can become a checkeristic
Christopher Columbus and do your own exploring.

A CHOICE ENDING

(BLACK)

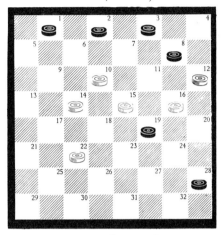

(WHITE)

PROBLEM NUMBER 76
By Tom Wiswell
BLACK: 1, 2, 3, 8, 19, 28
WHITE: 10, 12, 14, 15, 16, 22
TERMS: White to play; what result?

SOLUTION

16–11——A, 3-7!!——B, C, 11-4, 1-6!!!——D, 10-3——
E, 6-10——F, 14-7, 2-25——F, drawn.

A——White is about to gain a man and, of course, hopes to win the game.

B——But this unusual combination saves the day for Black. 1-6 now won't work: 1-6, 10-1, 3-7, 12-3, White wins.

C——28-32 was played in the actual game and White won as follows: 28-32, 11-4, 32-27, 22-17, 27-23, 15-11, 23-18, 4-8!, 18-9, 10-6 (or 10-7), 1-10, 11-7, White wins.

D——White can take his choice and Black draws, regardless.

E——Because 10-1, 7-10, etc. draws, as above.

F——The game as shown in note C was played at the New York Club on July 22, 1969, and I demonstrated the draw after the game. I later set the position up for several experts (at the diagram) and asked them what it was, and most of them declared it a win for White! They all saw the difficult win, but not the "simple" draw! Yes, Checkers is a simple game, made up of many simplicities.

COLLABORATION

(BLACK)

(WHITE)

PROBLEM NUMBER 77
By Tom Wiswell
BLACK: 2, 18, 28 KINGS
        12, 23, 31
WHITE: 10, 17, 19, 30, 32
       KING 11
TERMS: White to play and
       win

SOLUTION

11–16, 18-22, 16-20, 23-16, 20-11, 22-26——A, 30-23,
31-27, 23-18——B, 27-23, 18-14——C, 23-18, 17-13, 18-9,
13-6, 2-9, 10-6——D, 9-14, 6-2, 14-18, 2-6, 18-22, 6-10,
22-26, 10-15, 26-31, 15-19, 31-26, 19-24——E, 26-22, 11-
16, 12-19, 24-15, White wins.

A——Black's best hope to draw; if 31-27, 32-23, 28-32, 23-
18, 32-27, 17-13, 27-23, 18-14, 23-18, 10-7, 18-9, 13-6, 2-9,
7-2, etc., White wins.

B——If 23-19, 27-23, 19-15 (11-16, 23-18), 23-18, 10-7,
18-22, 17-13, 12-16, drawn.

C——If 17-14, 23-19, 11-16, 19-23, 16-20, 12-8, 32-27,
23-32, 20-24, 8-12, draws.

D—Black has "the move" but White plans to change it—
with the help of one of Black's own men! This is "forced
collaboration."

E——Using the man on square 28 as a "backstop"—adding
insult to injury. Not difficult, perhaps, but instructive and
useful.

IN AGAIN, OUT AGAIN

(BLACK)

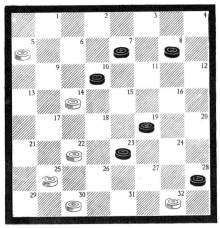

(WHITE)

PROBLEM NUMBER 78
By Tom Wiswell
BLACK: 7, 8, 10, 19, 23, 28
WHITE: 5, 14, 22, 25, 30, 32
TERMS: White to play and win

SOLUTION

22–17——A, 10-15——B, 5-1, 19-24, 1-6, 7-11, 6-10, 15-19, 10-7——C, 11-16, 7-3, 8-12, 30-26——D, 23-30, 3-7——D, 30-21, 14-10, 21-14, 7-2, 14-7, 2-27, 12-16, 27-24, 19-23, 24-19, 23-26, 19-12, 26-31, 12-16, 31-26, 16-19, 26-31, 19-15, White wins.

A——Necessary, if 14-9, 10-15, 9-6, 7-11, 6-2, 19-24, 5-1 (2-7, 23-26), 11-16, 2-7, 15-19, etc. Black draws, with care.

B——Black must now prepare to get his men out of the way and try to break the White bridge; it is his only logical continuation.

C——If 30-26, 23-30, 10-7, 30-21, 7-23, 24-27, etc., draws for Black.

D——The "in-and-out" shot, one of the basic ideas utilized by composers, problemists, and crossboard players. Black may vary from the above play, but White wins, regardless. Norman Wexler described this as "one of the best problems I have ever seen."

OLD GAME, NEW TWIST

(BLACK)

(WHITE)

PROBLEM NUMBER 79
By Tom Wiswell
BLACK: 2, 5, 8, 17, 21, 28
WHITE: 10, 14, 15, 18, 32
KING 9
TERMS: White to play and win

SOLUTION

9–13, 17-22, 13-17, 22-25——A, 17-22, 25-29——B, 15-11, 8-15, 18-11, 21-25, 11-8, 25-30, 8-4, 30-25, 14-9——C, 25-18, 4-8, 5-14, 10-7, 2-11, 8-22, 29-25, 22-29, 14-18, 29-25——D, White wins.

A——If 22-26, 17-22, 21-25 (26-31, 15-11), 22-31, 25-30, 31-27, 30-26, 14-9, 5-23, 27-18, 26-31, 18-22, 8-12, 15-11, 12-16, 11-8, 16-19, 8-4, 19-23, 22-25, 31-27 (31-26, 25-30), 4-8, 27-24, 25-30, etc., White wins.

B——If 25-30, 15-11, 8-15, 18-11, etc., White wins.

C——This basic type of "man-down" win is instructive and eludes many students and beginners in actual crossboard play. It often comes up with pieces on 32 and 28 as in the above position. The timing, of course, has to be right, as well as "the move," which is much the same thing.

D——Based on a game played at the New York Club and missed by White—but his name is Legion.

SUDDEN DEATH

(BLACK)

(WHITE)

PROBLEM NUMBER 80
By Tom Wiswell
BLACK: 3, 5, 9, 13, 23
WHITE: 11, 18, 22, 30, 31
TERMS: White to play and
win

SOLUTION

18–15, 9-14, 15-10, 14-17, 22-18——A, 5-9——B, 10-6,
17-22——C, 6-1, 13-17, 18-14!!——D, 9-18, 1-6, 17-21
——E, 11-7, 3-10, 6-15, 21-25, 30-21, 23-26, 15-10, 26-30,
10-14, 18-23, 14-18——F, White wins.

A——If 31-26, 23-27, 10-6, 27-31, 6-1, 5-9, 1-6, 9-14, 6-10
(6-9, 17-21), 31-27, etc., draws. (If, at this point, White
plays 11-7, 17-21, Black wins.)

B——Otherwise, White wins with 18-14.

C——Of course, Black plans to line up by 13-17 and 9-13,
and draw.

D——But White produces a "spoiler" that leaves the enemy
in complete disarray; though a man down, White wins easily.

E——If 23-27, 31-24, 18-23, 11-7, 3-10, 6-15, etc., White
wins.

F——Based on 10-14, 23-19, 14-18 and won by the writer in
a small match with Herman Schecter on August 21, 1971.
Herman is a little-known star (nationally) who ranks among
the top ten in New York; he is a superb crossboard player
who really looks them over, and this makes him an excellent
sparring partner who can beat the best of them on occasion.

CHAIN REACTION

(BLACK)

(WHITE)

PROBLEM NUMBER 81
By Tom Wiswell
BLACK: 13, 23, 28 KINGS
1, 6, 10
WHITE: 7, 25, 29, 32
KINGS 22, 31
TERMS: White to play and
win

SOLUTION

7-2——A, 1-5——B, 2-9, 5-14, 22-18, 14-17——C, 18-27, 17-21, 25-22——D, 21-25, 22-18, 25-22, 18-15——E, 10-19, 27-23——E, 19-26, 29-25——F, 22-29, 31-22, 13-17, 22-13, 29-25, 13-17——G, White wins.

A——Of course, if 7-3, 23-26, White's win disappears.

B——If 6-9, 22-18, White wins.

C——Black hopes to regain the man—and does, but loses in the process.

D——31-26, 21-23, 27-18, 10-6, 18-14, 6-1, 29-25, 1-5, etc., only draws.

E——White's strategy is now revealed in all its glory!

F——The "spread eagle" theme is utilized once again, but did *you* see the idea in the beginning? Now go over the entire solution again.

G——A favorite of New Jersey Champ, Jack Botte, of Jersey City. Jack is a frequent visitor to the New York Club and holds his own with the best of them. Problems are his specialty, "especially," he says, "when they end like this."

109

TOUR DE FORCE

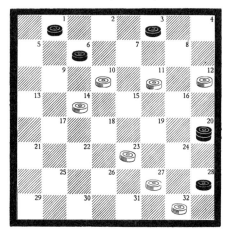

(BLACK)

(WHITE)

PROBLEM NUMBER 82

By Tom Wiswell

BLACK: 1, 3, 6, 28 KING 20

WHITE: 10, 11, 12, 14, 23, 27, 32

TERMS: White to play and win

SOLUTION

11-7——A, 6-15, 7-2, 15-18——B, 14-10, 18-22, 2-7, 22-26——C, 27-24——E, 20-18, 12-8, 3-12, 10-6, 1-10, 7-30, 12-16, 30-26——F, 16-19, 32-27, 28-32, 27-24, 19-28, 26-23, White wins.

A——The only move to win; against anything else Black draws, at least.

B——If 20-16, 27-24, 16-20 (16-11, 23-19, 15-18, 19-15, White wins), 23-19, 20-27, 19-10, 27-23, 14-9, 23-18, 2-7, 18-15 (or 18-14), 9-6, 15-18, 6-2, 18-14 (18-15, 7-11), 12-8, 3-12, 7-3, etc., White wins.

C——If 1-5——D, 7-2, 22-26, 2-6, 26-31 (or 26-30), 27-24, 20-18, 10-7, White wins.

D——If 22-25, 7-11, 25-30, 11-15, 30-25, 15-18, 20-16, 10-7, etc., White wins.

E——Black has been forced into the shot, but winds up with "the move"; however, one of the most basic themes saves the win for White.

F——I continue the solution solely for the benefit of the student.

NO PLACE TO GO

PROBLEM NUMBER 83
By Al Sprangle and Tom Wiswell

BLACK: 1, 3, 6, 9, 20 KING 32

WHITE: 11, 12, 13, 17, 21 KINGS 8, 28

TERMS: White to play and win

SOLUTION

11–7——A, 3-10, 8-11, 20-24——B, 28-19, 10-14, 17-10, 6-24, 13-6, 1-10, 12-8——C, 32-27, 8-3——C, 27-23, 3-7, 10-14, 11-15, 23-19, 7-10——D, White wins.

A——An instructive end-game from 10-15, 21-17, 15-18; White returns the extra man and just barely forces a pretty win.

B——If 32-27, 28-24, etc., White wins, and against 9-14, 11-7, 10-15, 17-10, 15-18, 13-9! wins quickly. (Tom Wiswell and Dave Midler)

C——White has his eye on the man on square 10, although the Black King on square 32 *seems* to be in time in coming to the rescue.

D——Al Sprangle is one of New York's "top ten" and a hardy crossboard performer. He is typical of the big city breed—perhaps not so well known outside of Manhattan, but capable of holding his own with the best of them. The fact that he "looks them over" makes him doubly dangerous in a tight spot.

NEW YORK vs. CONNECTICUT

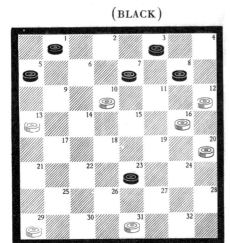

(BLACK)

(WHITE)

PROBLEM NUMBER 84
By Harold Freyer
BLACK: 1, 3, 5, 7, 8, 23
WHITE: 10, 12, 13, 16, 20, 29, 31
TERMS: White to play and draw

SOLUTION

10-6——A, 1-10, 29-25, 8-11, 25-21, 10-15, 21-17, 15-18 ——B, 17-14, 18-22, 13-9, 22-25, 9-6, 25-29, 6-2, 29-25, 14-10——C, 7-14, 16-7, 3-10, 2-6——D, drawn.

A——Although White is one ahead, this is his only move to draw and, in the end, he just barely scrapes through.

B——Black appears to be on his way to victory, but White has an "escape hatch" prepared; 15-19 is no better than the text.

C——The saving link on White's drawing board, and it brings the game to an instructive finish.

D——Harold Freyer (White) *vs.* Howard Peck in a short match played during 1969 that ended with all games drawn. Harold has been among America's top ten for more than thirty years and back in 1938 tied with the writer for the New York Masters' Championship. Our tourney record is all even, thanks to my good fortune.

JUMPING TO A CONCLUSION

(BLACK)

(WHITE)

PROBLEM NUMBER 85
By Tom Wiswell

BLACK: 1, 3, 5 KINGS 22, 24, 27

WHITE: 14, 17, 23, 32 KINGS 4, 10, 13

TERMS: White to play and win

SOLUTION

4–8——A, 27-9 (3-12, 32-28), 13-6, 3-12, 32-28, 22-13, 28-19, 13-17 (or 5-9), 10-7, 1-10, 7-21——B, White wins.

A——The key to the winning combination; nothing else works. For example: 32-28, 27-9, 13-6, 22-13, 28-19, 3-7, etc., draws. It is a jumping contest from now on.

B——The first move is the clue that the solver must spot in this composition. It created considerable interest in a solving contest held at The Chess and Checker Club of New York, and only winner Gerard LeClair was able to arrive at the correct solution in under five minutes. Get up a problem-solving contest in your group or club some time and see who will be the first one to solve a tough, new problem *without touching the pieces.* Remember: THE CHAMP DOESN'T TOUCH THEM UNTIL HE SEES IT AND THE CHUMP DOESN'T SEE IT UNTIL HE TOUCHES THEM!

PERPETUAL MOTION

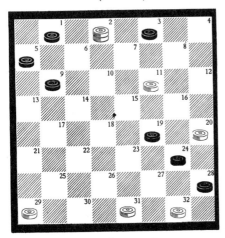

(BLACK)

(WHITE)

PROBLEM NUMBER 86
By Tom Wiswell
BLACK: 1, 3, 5, 9, 19, 24-28
WHITE: 11, 20, 29, 31, 32 KING 2
TERMS: White to play and draw

SOLUTION

11-7, 3-10, 2-6, 10-15 (or 10-14), 6-13, 5-9, 13-6, 1-10, 20-16, 19-23, 16-11, 15-18, 11-7, 10-14, 29-25——A, 14-17 ——B, 25-21, 17-22, 7-2, 22-25, 2-7, 18-22, 7-11, 25-30, 11-15——C, 30-25, 15-19——D, 23-27, 32-23, 22-26, 31-22, 25-27, 21-17, 27-31, 19-23, 28-32, 23-19, 24-28 (if 32-28, 19-23), 19-23, 31-27, 23-19——E, drawn.

A——7-2, 23-27, 32-23, 18-27, 2-6, 27-32, 6-10, 14-17, 10-14, 17-21, 14-18, 32-27, etc., Black wins.

B——If 23-27, 32-23, 18-27, 25-22, drawn.

C——NOT 11-16, 30-26, 16-20, 23-27, 32-23, 26-19, 20-27, 28-32, trapped!

D——If 15-18, 23-27, 32-23, 25-29, 18-25, 29-22, 23-19, 28-32, 19-15, 32-28, 15-10, 24-27, etc., Black wins.

E——One holds off three in this situation and even though the King on 27 can leave the double corner he cannot in any way damage White because the King on 23 effectively ties up his two companions.

THE NUTMEG CHAMPION

(BLACK)

(WHITE)

PROBLEM NUMBER 87
By Tom Wiswell and
Howard Peck
BLACK: 1, 4, 6, 12, 16, 18
KING 32
WHITE: 21, 28, 29, 30, 31
KING 7
TERMS: White to play and
draw

SOLUTION

7–11, 16-20, 30-26, 32-27——A, 31-24, 20-27, 11-15, 18-23
——B, 26-19, 6-10——B, 15-6, 1-10, 29-25, 27-31, 25-22,
31-27, 22-18, 27-24, 19-16——C, 12-19, 21-17, 24-27, 18-15
——D, etc., drawn.

A——Black has nothing better at this stage—or has he?

B——These moves leave Black in a position that *appears*
to win, but there is more here than meets the eye.

C——A timely maneuver that comes up from several openings and one that may save you from defeat in the future.

D——Based on 10-15, 21-17, 9-13, played in a ten-game
match with Mr. Peck, the former Connecticut State Champion, a strong crossboard performer. Although I had several
settings to my credit, on this occasion Howard held me even
by 3-3-4 and greatly impressed Harold Freyer, who was an
interested onlooker. This game took place July 27, 1968,
at the rooms of The Chess and Checker Club of New York.

EXHIBITIONIST

(BLACK)

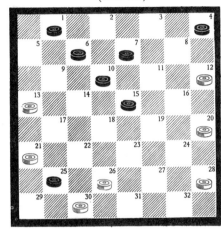

(WHITE)

PROBLEM NUMBER 88
By Tom Wiswell

BLACK: 1, 4, 6, 7, 10, 15, 25

WHITE: 12, 13, 20, 21, 26, 28, 30

TERMS: White to play and win

SOLUTION

21–17——A, 25-29, 26-23, 1-5, 23-19, 15-24, 28-19, 5-9 ——B, 20-16——C, 9-14, 19-15——C, 14-21, 15-11—— D, etc., White wins.

A——Note how well White forces the play from here to the end.

B——If 7–11, 19-16, 11-15, 12-8, 4-11, 16-7, etc., White wins.

C——These moves took my opponent by surprise, but I had planned them from the time I went 21-17 at the diagrammed position.

D——Sometimes I can give a perfect example of good end-game technique in one of my exhibitions, and this was the case in this Single Corner ending played at Oswego, New York, on August 4, 1966, at a display arranged by young John Herberger and veteran Wesley Nickerson. Later I published this position in *Elam's Checkerboard* under the very appropriate title of *Oswego A-Go-Go*.

THE NAKED EYE

(BLACK)

(WHITE)

PROBLEM NUMBER 89
By Tom Wiswell
BLACK: 2, 4, 26 KINGS 15, 17, 25

WHITE: 10, 12, 14, 16, 20, 24, 27 KING 28

TERMS: White to play and win

SOLUTION

28–32——A, 15-6 14-10——B, 6-15, 12-8——C, 4-11, 16-7——C, 2-11, 20-16——D, 11-20, 27-23——D, 20-27, 23-18——E, 15-22, 32-14——F, White wins.

A——Sometimes you can be two men ahead and still fail to see a winning combination, either because the win is not there, or you are unable to see the "clearing" process that makes the win visible to the naked eye.

B——The proper sacrifice of your extra men brings about the desired result, as you will soon see.

C——Watch this combination closely, since it comes up frequently in play.

D——Now the mechanics of the win are visible, even to the amateur.

E——The "simple" idea that was hidden by all the complicated trappings.

F——Set the men up again and train yourself to see the entire solution without touching the pieces. Do this in each problem to improve your "naked eye" power.

117

THE PIN

(BLACK)

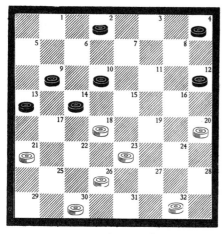

(WHITE)

PROBLEM NUMBER 90
By Tom Wiswell
BLACK: 2, 4, 9, 10, 12, 13, 14
WHITE: 18, 20, 21, 23, 26, 30, 32
TERMS: White to play and win

SOLUTION

32–28——A, 4-8, 28-24, 8-11, 24-19——B, 13-17——C, 20-16!——D, 11-20, 19-16——D, 12-19, 23-16, 14-23, 21-7, 2-11, 26-19——E, White wins.

A——NOT 32-27, 12-16, 20-11, 10-15, 26-22, 15-19, 23-16, 14-32, and the tables are turned.

B——Black expects to draw, but White has a definite blueprint for victory, as the next few moves will show.

C——These moves reveal White's strategy; if 19-16, 12-19, 23-7, 2-11, then White lacks a satisfactory waiting move for a win, but 26-22, 17-26, 30-23, 10-15, 20-16, etc., draws.

D——I surprised my exhibition opponent with these moves.

E——And the Black piece is "pinned," a manuever that is often overlooked in crossboard play. This ending came up from 9-14, 22-18, 5-9.

STOP, THIEF!

(BLACK)

(WHITE)

PROBLEM NUMBER 91
By Tom Wiswell

BLACK: 1, 3, 18, 20, 21,
        23 KING 12

WHITE: 5, 13, 14, 15, 17,
        27, 29, 32

TERMS: White to play and
        win

SOLUTION

15–11——A, 12-16——B, 13-9——C, 16-7, 14-10——C,
7-14, 17-10, 3-8, 9-6——D, 8-11, 6-2——D, 11-16, 2-7——
D, 16-19, 32-28——E, 23-32, 10-6, 1-10, 7-16——F, White
wins.

A——Only move to win; if 13-9, 3-7, etc., draws; if 15-10,
12-16, etc., draws.

B——Hoping to steal the man on 27. Note that if this King
were a man the game would be a draw! The power of the
common man!!

C——Timing and planning will prevent the "big theft."

D——Or 10-7. Watch how Black's plans are foiled in the
nick of time.

E——From an *Octopus* ending, believe it or not.

F——This could have come from a game with Howard Peck,
but the Cheshire champ avoided this variation and drew the
game and the match on May 18, 1969.

THE TRIANGLE

(BLACK)

(WHITE)

PROBLEM NUMBER 92
By Tom Wiswell
BLACK: 1, 2, 6, 8, 16, 25, 28
WHITE: 5, 9, 13, 14, 17, 21, 30, 32
TERMS: White to play and win

SOLUTION

14–10——A, 6-15, 17-14, 2-7——B, 21-17——C, 25-29, 30-25——C, 29-22, 9-6——D, 1-10, 13-9——E, 22-6, 5-1, 10-17, 1-10——F, White wins.

A——While examining a position at the New York Checker Club this win flashed through my mind in a matter of seconds; every player has experienced this thrilling phenomenon, although all too seldom, as a rule.

B——If 16-19, 14-10, 19-23, 9-6, 2-9, 13-6, 15-19 (23-27, 32-23, 28-32, 6-2, White wins), 6-2, 19-24, 21-17, 25-29, 2-7, 24-27, 10-6, 1-10, etc., White wins.

C——These moves are very forceful and lead to a fine coup.

D——Making way for the King and the necessary "waiting" move.

E——The basic mechanism which I saw at the diagrammed position; do not sell your imagination short when analyzing a game—anything is possible: Dream the impossible dream, fight the unbeatable foe!

F——Played December 8, 1967 at The Chess and Checker Club of New York.

CHECKERBOARD CHOREOGRAPHY

(BLACK)

(WHITE)

PROBLEM NUMBER 93
By Tom Wiswell
BLACK: 1, 2, 3, 12, 18, 21
KING 19
WHITE: 5, 9, 10, 14, 20,
25, 26, 27, 30
TERMS: White to play and
win

SOLUTION

9–6, 2-9, 27-23, 18-27, 20-16, 9-18, 10-6, 1-10, 26-23, 19-26, 30-7, 3-10, 5-1, 12-19, 1-6, 21-30, 6-31——A, White wins.

A——Here is another by the author that you might enjoy:
 BLACK: 8, 12, 16, 19, 20, 23
 WHITE: 28, 31, 32 KING 22
 TERMS: White to play and draw
 SOLUTION

22–18, 8-11, 18-27, 11-15, 31-26, 15-18, 28-24——A, 19-28, 26-23, 18-22, 23-19, 16-23, 27-25, 12-16, 25-22, 16-19, 22-18, 20-24, 18-15, 19-23, 15-19, 23-26, 19-16, etc., drawn.

A——If 27-24, 20-27, 32-14, 19-24, Black wins. This sacrifice leads to a cleancut draw and a familiar theme with which you should be well acquainted.

THE WAITING GAME

(BLACK)

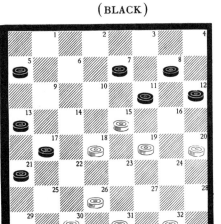

(WHITE)

PROBLEM NUMBER 94
By Tom Wiswell
BLACK: 5, 7, 8, 11, 12, 13, 17, 21
WHITE: 15, 18, 19, 20, 26, 30, 31, 32
TERMS: White to play and win

SOLUTION

19–16, 12-19, 26-22, 17-26, 30-16, 8-12, 15-8, 12-19, 8-3
——A, 7-10, 3-7, 10-14, 18-9, 5-14, 7-11, 19-23, 20-16!
——B, 14-17 (if 21-25, 11-15, etc., White wins), 11-15, 23-26, 31-22, 17-26, 15-18——C, White wins.

A——If 18-14, 7-11, 8-3, 11-15, 3-7, 19-23, 7-10, 15-18, 20-16 (10-15, 18-22, etc., drawn), 21-25, 16-11, 25-29, 11-7, 29-25, 7-3, 25-21, etc., draws.

B——The waiting move that clinches the win for White. This type of play often eludes the student, who is more apt to play 11-15, 23-26, 31-22, 14-18, etc., which is only a draw.

C——Illustrating the value of that timely waiting move in a critical end-game position. Keep a sharp lookout for such subtle plays and they will help you win many an otherwise drawn game. Missing a win may be as bad as losing a game if your opponent scores in the next frame, a fact you should always keep in mind.

NINETEEN MOVES

(BLACK)

(WHITE)

PROBLEM NUMBER 95
By Tom Wiswell
BLACK: 1, 3, 4, 12, 18
KINGS 17, 19, 25
WHITE: 5, 10, 11, 15, 20,
27, 32 KING 2
TERMS: White to play and
draw

SOLUTION

27–23, 19-26——A, 20-16, 12-19, 10-7, 3-10, 15-6, 1-10, 2-7!——B, drawn.

A——If 18-27, 32-16, 12-19, 10-7, 3-10, 15-6, 1-10, 11-8, 4-11, 2-7, etc., is a fast, clean-cut draw.

B——Black actually has nineteen possible moves (and is three men ahead), yet cannot prevent White from drawing. In this position the threat is truly equal to the execution. While this is a composition, it is based on an actual ending from a New York Knock-out tourney. If you get into an unusual position in a game—don't forget this—find a good setting for the idea and submit it to one of the checker magazines as a problem; in that way others will also benefit from your experience and you will be more apt to remember the idea when you again encounter it in crossboard play.

THE MUSIC MAN

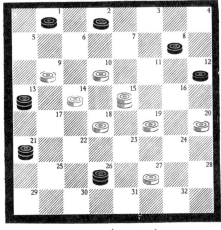

(BLACK)

(WHITE)

PROBLEM NUMBER 96
By Anthony Petronella
BLACK: 1, 2, 8, 12 KINGS
13, 21, 26
W ITE: 9, 10, 14, 18, 19,
20, 27 KING 15
TE MS: White to play and
win

SOLUTION

10–7——A, 2-11, 14-10——A, 13-6, 20-16——A, 11-20,
27-24, 20-27, 19-16, 12-19, 15-22, 6-15, 18-4——B, 1-5,
4-8, 5-9, 8-11, 9-13, 11-15, 21-17, 22-18, 17-21, 18-14——
C, 13-17, 15-19——C, 17-22, 19-23——C, 22-25, 23-26,
25-29, 26-30, 29-25, 14-18——D, White wins.

A——Black's three Kings look ominous, but this neat combination, and an instructive ending, carry the day for White.

B——And we have a "two by two" that terminates in a "familiar theme."

C——Once again the "American Position" comes to the rescue.

D——Anthony Petronella, the author, is a master violinist who has played with some of the best orchestras in the country—and he is just as skilled at the checkerboard. He collects rare violins, as well as rare checker books!

TRIPLE THREAT

(BLACK)

(WHITE)

PROBLEM NUMBER 97
By Tom Wiswell
BLACK: 3, 15, 16, 20, 22
             KINGS 5, 17
WHITE: 9, 11, 12, 23, 27,
           28, 32 KING 13
TERMS: White to play and
           win

SOLUTION

28–24———A, 5-14, 23-19, 16-23, 27-9, 20-27, 32-23, 17-14
———B, 9-5———C, 22-26, 11-7!———D, 3-10, 12-8, 26-31
———E, 8-3, 31-27, 3-7, 27-18, 13-9———F, 15-19, 5-1, 14-5,
7-16, White wins.

A——These are the only moves to win, and they lead to an
unusual and instructive ending.

B——Black, a man down, has his eye on the piece on square
23.

C——If 9-6, 22-26, etc., only draws.

D——13-9 (5-1, 26-31), 14-17, 5-1, 26-31, 1-5, 17-21,
draws, but 17-22, 11-7, 3-10, 23-18, loses for Black and so
does 31-27, 9-6, 27-18, 6-10, etc. White wins.

E——If 15-18, 13-9, 18-27, 9-18, etc., White wins.

F——White's "grand design" from the start, and based on
an actual ending from "The Single Corner." Black can play
otherwise, but to no avail.

PLANNING BOARD

(BLACK)

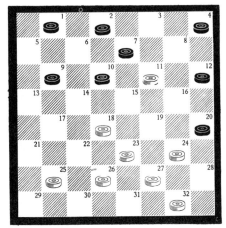

(WHITE)

PROBLEM NUMBER 98
By Tom Wiswell
BLACK: 1, 2, 4, 7, 9, 10, 12, 20
WHITE: 11, 18, 23, 24, 25, 26, 27, 32
TERMS: White to play and draw

SOLUTION

25–21——A, 7-16, 18-14, 9-18——B, 23-7, 2-11, 26-23—— C, 1-6——D, 21-17, 6-10, 17-13, 4-8——E, 13-9, 10-14—— F, 9-6, 14-17, 6-2, 17-22, 2-7, 22-26, 23-19——G, 16-23, 27-18, 20-27, 7-16——G, 12-19, 32-16, drawn.

A——Although it is not apparent at this stage, White has a "grand design" on the planning board; watch the time-table!

B——10-17, 21-5, etc., presents no problems for White.

C——Although White is one down, he has the situation well in hand.

D——1-5, 21-17, 5-9, 17-13, 11-15, 13-6, 16-19, 23-16, 12-28, 6-2, 4-8, 2-7, 8-12, 7-11, 15-19, 11-15, 19-24, 27-23, 24-27, 15-19, 27-31, 23-18, drawn.

E——Note how Black also times his moves to counter White's plans.

F——Free to get a King, and score—so it seems on the surface.

G——The culmination of the plan begun at the diagram.

COMPOUND INTEREST

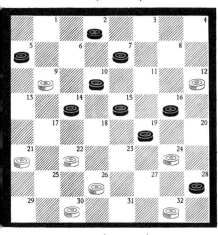

(BLACK)

(WHITE)

PROBLEM NUMBER 99
By Tom Wiswell
BLACK: 2, 5, 7, 10, 14, 15, 16, 19, 28
WHITE: 9, 12, 21, 22, 24, 26, 30, 32
TERMS: White to play and win

SOLUTION

21–17——A, 14-21, 12-8, 5-14, 30-25——B, 21-30, 8-3, 30-23, 22-18, 15-22, 24-6, 2-9, 3-12——C, White wins.

A——The quiet before the storm; things are going to happen!

B——Leading into the compound stroke; very interesting.

C——Here is an ending from an entirely different point of view:

> BLACK: 6, 16
> WHITE: 32 KING 29
> TERMS: Black to play; what result?
> ### SOLUTION

6–10, 29-25, 10-15, 25-22, 15-19, 22-26, 19-24, 26-31, 24-28 (Presto! changing "the move"), 31-26, 16-19, 32-27, 28-32, 27-24! (Presto! changing everything), 19-28, 26-23, White wins.

JIG-SAW PUZZLE

(BLACK)

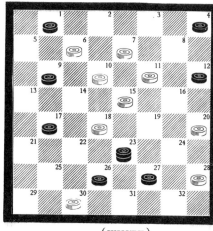

(WHITE)

PROBLEM NUMBER 100
By Author Unknown
BLACK: 1, 4, 9, 12, 17, 26, 27 KING 23
WHITE: 6, 7, 10, 11, 15, 18, 20, 28, 30
TERMS: White to play and win

SOLUTION

30–25——A, 23-14, 11-8——A, 4-18, 20-16——A, 12-19, 7-2——A, 14-7, 2-11, 1-10, 11-15!——B, White wins.

A—— These moves lead to an extremely novel and sensational win that should please student and expert alike. "Always look for the unexpected" is an old bromide, but, in this case, it really describes the situation.

B——What would you do if your opponent executed a coup like this?

The score is seven to three, but the three win out against the seven. Black has thirteen choices, all bad: If 27-32, 15-24, White wins; if 27-31, 15-24, White wins; if 26-31, 15-24, White wins; if 26-30, 15-31, White wins; if 19-23, 15-24, White wins; if 19-24, 15-31, White wins; if 18-23, 15-15, White wins; if 18-22, 15-31, 22-29, 31-15, White wins; if 17-22, 15-31, 22-29, 31-13, White wins; if 17-21, 15-13, White wins; if 9-13, 15-6, White wins; if 9-14, 15-6 and if 10-14, 15-6, White wins.

DOUBLE AGENT

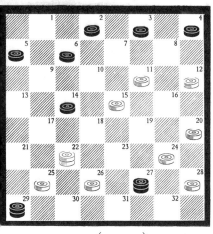

(WHITE)

(BLACK)

PROBLEM NUMBER 101
By Tom Wiswell
BLACK: 2, 3, 4, 5, 6, 14
          KINGS 27, 29
WHITE: 11, 12, 15, 20,
          24, 25, 26, 28
          KING 22
TERMS: White to play and
          win

SOLUTION

20–16——A, 27-20, 28-24——B, 20-27, 12-8——B, 3-19, 11-7——C, 2-18, 22-31——D, 29-22, 26-1——E, White wins.

A——The only move to win, and it leaves no doubt about the outcome.

B——Getting the pieces in the right formation for the "big blow."

C——Leads to the "double stroke," with the King on square 22 serving as a capturing agent and then acting as the foundation for the second triple.

D——Triple number one!

E——Triple number two! Of course, White has "the move" on the two single men and easily brings matters to a quick conclusion. Try your hand at composing a stroke, but make sure the idea is well hidden and, above all, make your setting as natural-looking as possible. The fewer Kings the better.

129

A Note on The Chess and Checker Club of New York

America's largest and best-known chess and checker club is located at 212 West 42nd Street, in the heart of New York's famed Times *Square* (naturally), and is officially known as The Chess and Checker Club of New York. For fully a quarter of a century the greats and near-greats of the checker and chess world have made this club, conducted by John Fursa, the genial MAJOR DOMO of this establishment, their headquarters when in the big city.

On almost any day of the week, and indeed at almost any hour of the day, one may find a hundred players busily engaged in checking kings or pushing checkers, quite oblivious to all the bustle and excitement of the "Gay White Way" just outside the club's windows. In fact, on one memorable occasion some years ago, a fire broke out at the club and the firemen came and put out the blaze while most of the players went right on with their games, paying not the least attention to the city's brave smoke-eaters.

Although the club's chess players outnumber the checkerists and have won laurels for the club, it is the checker players who have brought world fame to the club by their achievements across the board. The club's checker team has won the United States and North American team titles, and in the spring of 1968 traveled across the Atlantic to Belfast in Northern Ireland, where they won the International team title (see photo). After more than a dozen important matches, the club's team remains still undefeated and untied!

Daily battles between checker greats are common sights and single-knockouts are staged almost monthly. Early in 1951 young Maurice Chamblee, who in 1950 had won the American Tourney at Paxton, Illinois, played his challenge match for the world match title against the then World 3-Move Champion, Walter Hellman, in the rooms of the club. The writer himself has trained for many of his important matches by practice heats at the club with such noted New York stars as Morris Krantz, George Moore, Ed Scheidt, Abe Bernstein, Jack Botte, and many others of like calibre.

On any day, and especially on weekend evenings, one may encounter such celebrities of the checker world as Harold Freyer, Norman or Paul Wexler, Dave Midler, Arthur Gladstone, Jack Botte, Louis Burt, Jules Leopold, Dr. J. Belinkoff, Jimmy Ricca, Herman Schecter, Walter Michaelis, Leonard Porter, Professor Arnold Gallub, Al Sprangle, Fred Kritzler, Ben Boland, and indeed, scores of other notables of the checker-playing fraternity. This club is indeed the Mecca of checkers in the East.

The late Leonard Rosenfield, the boy genius, made many notable records here and remained undefeated against some of New York's strongest match talent. Unfortunately, his brilliant budding career, which had shown such great promise for national checker honors, came to a tragic end when he was 17, long before he had reached his peak as a player.

The invincible Dr. Marion F. Tinsley, for many years holder of many of the world's checker championship titles, generously treated the club's members to a rare spectacle some years ago. On a quiet Sunday afternoon Dr. Tinsley staged a ten-game exhibition match in the club's spacious room with one of New York's brightest masters, Harold Freyer, who distinguished himself nobly by holding his great opponent to ten straight drawn games, a genuine checker treat that was indeed rare in the annals of checkers in the environs of the great metropolis. The never-to-be-forgotten Willie Ryan and his great contemporary, John Bradford, both now departed, often visited the club and participated in "knockout" tourneys. The club's mascot is the one-and-only Chris Nelson, of "Edinburgh" fame and long established in the lore of checker problems. This noted veteran is also a fine bridge player and often takes part in the club's bridge sessions.

The Chess and Checker Club of New York has witnessed some great events in its quarter-century history, and few indeed are the stars who have not crossed its threshold during this notable period—a truly "checkered" career of a justly famed checker club!

The Chess and Checkers Club of New York, International Team Champions

The five masters representing John Fursa's New York Club are, from left to right: Paul Wexler, Milton Loew, Jules Leopold, Jimmy Ricca, and Tom Wiswell, Captain.
Courtesy Belfast Telegraph

Statistics of Some Match Games

WORLD TEAM CHAMPIONSHIP MATCH

New York *vs.* Belfast, at Belfast, May 25, 1968

ROUND ONE

WINS	NEW YORK	DRAWS	BELFAST	WINS
1	Milton Loew	1	W. Doherty	0
1	Tom Wiswell	1	R. Surgenor	0
0	P. Wexler	2	A. Watson	0
0	Jules Leopold	2	M. Whiteside	0
1	Jimmy Ricca	1	W. Mills	0
—		—		—
3		7		0

ROUND TWO

WINS		DRAWS		WINS
2	Loew	0	J. Gilliland	0
0	Wiswell, Capt.	2	R. Surgenor	0
1	Wexler	1	A. Watson	0
0	Leopold	2	A. Whiteside	0
0	Ricca	2	W. Mills	0
—		—		—
3		7		0

Total: New York: 6 Wins   Belfast: 0 Wins   Drawn: 14
World Team Champions: The Chess and Checker Club of New York
       Director, New York Club: John Fursa
       Director, Belfast Club: Arthur Casey

MATCH COMMITTEE

PUBLICITY DIRECTORS

NORTH AMERICAN TEAM CHAMPIONSHIP MATCH

New York *vs.* Toronto, at Toronto, August 31, 1958

WINS	NEW YORK	DRAWS	TORONTO	WINS
0	Tom Wiswell	2	Norman Stephen	0
1	Bobby Martin	1	Prof. W. R. Fraser	0
1	Norman Wexler	1	E. V. Thompson	0
1	Vincent Ricciuti	1	E. H. Martin	0
0	Carm Avery	2	J. D. MacFarlane	0
0	Paul Wexler	2	F. E. Kendall	0
1	Allan Rupp	1	R. J. Campbell	0
2	Walter Michaelis	0	John Shore	0
—		—		—
6		10		0

Total: New York: 6 Wins   Toronto 0 Wins   Drawn: 10
North American Team Champions: The Chess and Checker Club of
    New York
Director, New York Club: John Fursa
Director, Toronto Club: A. S. Wheeler

U.S. TEAM CHAMPIONSHIP MATCH

New York *vs.* Jamaica, at New York, September 29, 1957

WINS	NEW YORK	DRAWS	JAMAICA	WINS
0	Tom Wiswell	2	Al Sprangle	0
0	Morris Krantz	2	Harold Freyer	0
1	Abe Bernstein	0	C. Albuquerque	1
1	V. Ricciuti	1	H. Schreibman	0
0	Gerard LeClair	1	Norman Wexler	1
1	Bill Gable	1	Barney Talis	0
1	Harry Koff	1	Abe Herman	0
0	Arthur Gladstone	2	Jack Cox	0
0	Carm Avery	2	J. Guiliani	0
0	Dr. Joe Kronman	2	Allan Rupp	0
—		—		—
4		14		2

Total: New York 4 Wins   Jamaica 2 Wins   Drawn: 14
U. S. Team Champions: The Chess and Checker Club of New York
Recapitulation of Three Matches: New York: 16 Wins
                                  Opponents: 2 Wins
                                  Drawn: 38

THE GAME OF CHECKERS

Whether on the desert waste or in the crowded town,
  In tents and camps and palaces it bears a like renown,
This game, if game it is, whose history we may scan
  Nearly as far adown the slope as history tells of man.
It seems almost an instinct which still, from age to age,
  Can charm the callow mind of youth and yet perplex the
    sage.
Complex, yet simple, open, close, 'tis near and also far,
  Elusive as a will-of-the-wisp and steadfast as a star.
'Tis light, 'tis dark, 'tis clear, 'tis obscure, a pleasure and a
    pain,
  And none this riddle truly reads save those that know
    the game;
And none have fully known the play in all its mazy past;
  For as well explore the depths of space as sound the
    depths of Draughts.
Queen Dameh, sweetest goddess of the Olympian mount
    of fame;
The common mind, in every age, has kindled at thy name:
  Thy victories are all bloodless; thy triumphs are of
    peace,
Thy captives form a willing train, they sigh not for release;
  And still thy kindly sceptre points beyond our
    shortening day
Where unknown millions yet unborn will gladly own thy
    sway.

                              Charles W. Monington—1906